Praise for *What Matters Most*

"*What Matters Most* shows you how to build a bridge between the person you now are and the person you really want to be by outlining a practical way to define your priorities and live accordingly."

—Tom Curley, *USA Today*

"A very important book—one that could change you and the way you think about things. Smith has given us the best work I've seen in a long, long while."

—Larry King

"Soul-deep truth for a society drowning in skin-deep role models."

—Dr. Denis Waitley, author of
The Psychology of Winning for the 21st Century

"Hyrum Smith has produced a deeply personal account helping readers to identify the core principles at the root of individual responsibilities and behavior. *What Matters Most* attests to the importance of self-discovery and its influence on our personal and professional lives."

—David H. Komansky,
Chairman and CEO, Merrill Lynch & Co., Inc.

"This is perhaps the finest book on time and personal management ever written. Its simple, practical, and elegant principles will revolutionize your life and bring it completely into balance while dramatically increasing your productivity."

—Brian Tracy, author of *Maximum Achievement*

"As the pace of the world continues to accelerate, it is increasingly difficult to focus on what really matters. This book is exactly what readers need to keep their values and priorities straight, and therefore realize their vision for the future."

—Rich DeVos, cofounder of Amway Corporation

"Knowing who you are and living consistently with that knowledge is the foundation of a successful life. In *What Matters Most,* Hyrum W. Smith provides a wonderful resource for understanding ourselves, our values, and our goals. Those who apply what he teaches will surely add value to their lives."

> —Stedman Graham, author of
> *You Can Make It Happen,*
> Chairman and CEO of S. Graham & Associates

"If you care about what really matters, read this book. Thoughtful and beautifully written. An enormous contribution to ethics, integrity, and the renewal of character."

> —Richard Carlson, author of
> *Don't Sweat the Small Stuff . . . and It's All Small Stuff*

"It's refreshing to find an author who so well maps out the territory we must traverse on life's journey. Hyrum Smith connects for us the interrelationships between beliefs, values, behaviors, planning, and action. He powerfully aids us with advice and tools for developing and continuously refreshing the personal values that drive our lives and lead to fundamental happiness and security."

> —Kirl L. Stromberg,
> retired director of Strategic Planning,
> American Association of Retired Persons (AARP)

"It's never too late to overcome your fears and begin living the life you've always wanted. *What Matters Most* outlines the steps to define, prioritize, and apply your values to every aspect of your life. The ideas and tools in this wonderful book can help you get from where you are to where you really want to be."

> —Ken Dychtwald, Ph.D.,
> president, Age Wave LLC and author of
> *Age Wave, Healthy Aging,* and *Age Power*

"If you're saying, 'I want my life to really count,' I know of no better recipe than to follow the step-by-step process Hyrum shares in this book."

> —Don Soderquist, Senior Vice Chairman,
> Wal-Mart Stores, Inc.

What
Matters
Most

The Power

What

of Living

Matters

Your Values

Most

HYRUM W. SMITH

SIMON & SCHUSTER
A VIACOM COMPANY

First published in Great Britain by Simon & Schuster UK Ltd, 2001
A Viacom Company

1 3 5 7 9 10 8 6 4 2

Simon & Schuster UK Ltd
Africa House
64-78 Kingsway
London WC2B 6AH

Simon & Schuster Australia
Sydney

A CIP catalogue record for this book is available from the British Library

ISBN 0-7432-0658-4

Printed and bound in Finland by WS Bookwell

The author gratefully acknowledges permission from the following
sources to reprint material in their control: Rodney Brainard, a Marble
Falls high school senior, for 'Paradox of Our Time', copyright © 1999 by
Rodney Brainard. All rights reserved. Dee Groberg for 'The Race'
copyright © 1974 by Dee Groberg. All rights reserved. HarperCollins
Publishers for Jerry C. Collins and Jerry I. Porras for *Built to Last:
Successful Habits of Visionary Companies*, copyright © 1994 by Jerry C.
Collins and Jerry I. Porras. Zondervan Publishing House for an excerpt
from 'Everyone's a Coach', by Don Shula and Ken Blanchard, copyright
© 1995 by Shula Enterprises and the Blanchard Family Partnership.

Acknowledgments

It would take many pages to list all the people who have in some way contributed to this book. It would require going back into the early days of my life and describing the impact that teachers, coaches, friends, family, etc., have had on me.

I will be concise in expressing my appreciation but would plead with you not to minimize the depth of my appreciation because of my brevity.

My deepest and heartfelt gratitude:

To Jerry Pulsipher for helping me write this book. Without Jerry the book would not exist. He played a major role in the creation of my first book and an even greater contribution here. His ability to help me focus my thoughts and ideas and then express them has been monumental.

To Greg Link and Annie Oswald for their untiring efforts in researching and verifying facts, editing the manuscript, and taking this work from the manuscript stage to the world.

To my wife and family who have stood by me in some of the most difficult times over the past several years as I have gone through the process of discovering what truly mattered most to me.

To hundreds of people at Franklin Covey who have made huge

contributions to make my dream of impacting the world a reality. In particular I must express my love and appreciation for the teaching consultants who leave their homes and family every week to take the message of *What Matters Most* to the world.

To hundreds of clients of our great company who have become and are some of my best friends. They have had a great impact on my life.

To Marion D. Hanks, a teacher, coach, mentor, friend, hero, and even a father to me.

To Ken Blanchard for his wonderful and unconditional love and respect. He has helped me through some challenging moments. His foreword for the book is most humbling. May we connect many days in the future.

Kahlil Gibran said, "In every man there is something wherein I may learn of him, and in that thing I am his pupil." Thank you all for touching my life.

To my wife, Gail, and our six children:

Glenna

Stacie

Sharwan

Joseph

Rebecca

Jacob

They have ordered their lives around
What Matters Most to them, and I deeply love
and respect all of them.

Contents

Contents

Foreword

by Ken Blanchard

When Hyrum Smith asked me if I would write a foreword to his new book, *What Matters Most*, I was thrilled. I am a big Hyrum Smith fan and have considered him a valued colleague since those early days when he conceived and helped bring forth the first Franklin Planner. His emphasis over the years has been consistent—going beyond mere time management to help people learn how to get in touch with and do something about the things in life that are most important to them.

I read *What Matters Most* while I was on a safari in Africa. The timing couldn't have been better. As I read the book, I realized I wasn't doing something to help Hyrum; he was doing something to help me.

In May I turned sixty. I told everyone that I was really excited about that milestone because I felt that the first fifty-nine years of my life were preparation for doing what the Lord really wanted me to do. Now I'm ready to contribute to the world. And I felt good about telling people that.

But the reality is that if you ask anyone, "Would you like to have made the world a better place for having been here?" they would all say, "Absolutely." And then if you ask them, "What's your game plan for making a difference and living consistently with your values?" they would look at you with a blank stare. I had that same blank look before I headed off on the safari. I knew I was excited about the next thirty-five or forty years, and I also knew that I could make a real difference. But I didn't have a vision as to how I might really do that nor a specific plan. I do now!

That's what this book, *What Matters Most*, can do for *you*. I was able to clarify what my mission in life is. I defined what my key values are and took a hard look at all the important roles I play. And then I clearly visualized what I would be doing on a day-to-day, week-to-week, month-to-month, and year-to-year basis in relation to the kind of life I want to live.

I got this focus from *What Matters Most*—a plan, a strategy, a way to make sure that every day I am being driven by more than just what is urgent. The telephone, voice mail, email, our "in basket," and all the other demands on us every day seem urgent. All these demands are undoubtedly important to other people. But unless you know where you are going, their demands can control your life. As a long-time colleague, Susan Fowler Woodring, has said many times, "People without goals will be used by those who have goals."

My goals are clear now. My strategy is clear. And I'm now even more excited about the next thirty-five to forty years than ever before. I want to thank you, Hyrum. You've made a difference in my life. And Hyrum can make a difference in your life when you read this book and use it. As Hyrum promises at the end of the book, may inner peace be your reward!

What Matters Most

Introduction:
Mount St. Helens, or Why You
Should Read This Book

Vision without action is a daydream. Action without vision is a nightmare.

—Japanese proverb

In the southwest corner of Washington State, there was once a beautiful, symmetrical mountain known as Mount St. Helens. It was one of a string of isolated volcanic peaks that run along the spine of the Cascade Range, from Canada south through Washington and Oregon into northern California. According to the geologists, these peaks were formed by violent eruptions in the past, but all were now considered extinct or dormant—until 1980.

Of these lofty peaks, Mount St. Helens is the youngest and the most beautiful to look at, or at least it was when I lived in Portland, Oregon, in the 1970s. We could look northward out of our window, across the Columbia River, on one of those rare clear days in the Pacific Northwest, and see St. Helens rising like a perfectly symmetrical cone, with smooth, forested slopes and a snow-capped summit. It looked like a classic picture postcard view of what a mountain should be. No one living in Portland at that time thought that our city's beautiful backdrop would ever change.

However, in January 1980, Mount St. Helens started to give off signals that it was alive but not feeling very well. It began to emit gas and steam from its cratered top, and the rumbling from deep in its core began to show on seismographs. Because of these signals, the geologists and gurus of volcanic mountains from all over the world flocked to southwestern Washington to see if they could predict what Mount St. Helens might do. The general consensus was that the mountain was waking from a centuries-long sleep, and powerful forces were beginning to move deep within her.

In February of that year a bulge began to grow on the northeastern slope of the mountain. The bulge grew at the rate of 9 feet per day, and by early May 1980 the bulge had expanded 400 feet. Because of the potential for a cataclysmic event, Dixie Lee Ray, the governor of Washington, issued an executive order requiring that everyone living within a twenty-mile radius of the base of Mount St. Helens immediately evacuate the area.

The danger was real, but it was interesting to note the reaction of some of the people who were asked to evacuate. Most of them just gathered their belongings and left the mountain, but there were several who were offended at the request to evacuate. One person in particular, the caretaker of Spirit Lake Lodge, was highly offended. Spirit Lake sat at the foot of the northeastern slope, just below the part of the mountain with the expanding bulge. The lodge was located on the northern shore of the lake, with a beautiful view of the mountain and the water of the lake reflecting an almost perfect mirror image of the peak.

The caretaker's name was Harry Truman—not *the* Harry Truman, the thirty-third president of the United States. As Mount St. Helens grew more dangerous, Mr. Truman became more vocal about his refusal to leave Spirit Lake Lodge. He became a kind of media celebrity, an eccentric man shouting defiance to the mountain. I witnessed one interview on national television, and I'll never forget what Harry Truman said. With a very belligerent look on his face he looked into the camera and said, "I've lived on this mountain for thirty-five years. No one knows more about this mountain than I do. It wouldn't dare blow up on me. I'm not leaving." So he stayed.

May 16 was a beautiful, sunny Friday, and the weather forecast was for more of the same through the weekend. Many of the people who had evacuated the mountain made a request to Governor Ray that they be allowed to return to their homes for the weekend, gather more of their personal belongings, and leave on Sunday or

Monday. The governor acquiesced, giving them twenty-four hours. She said, in effect, "You have from sundown Friday to sundown Saturday. Go back to the mountain, get your belongings, and get off the mountain by sundown Saturday night."

Several hundred people went back into the restricted area, spent the night, and then began to evacuate the mountain late Saturday afternoon as they had been instructed. Everyone left except eighty-four people. They looked at the weather and said to themselves, "You know, this is a marvelous weekend. What could possibly happen this weekend?" They decided to stay.

At about 6:30 on Sunday morning, May 18, Mount St. Helens blew up. It didn't just *erupt*. It blew up. And it blew up with such power and force that it lifted a cubic mile of mountain 60,000 feet in the air, turned it into burned sulfur and ash, and blew it around the world. In an instant the mountain lost the top one-third of its height. Thousands of acres of trees were blown down and incinerated by the force and heat of the winds that were generated. Spirit Lake was obliterated, and Harry Truman and his lodge were buried under hundreds of feet of rock and ash. Downwind for hundreds of miles to the northeast, volcanic ash fell like snow on homes, cars, and streets, and the sun was darkened. When the eruption subsided several days later, Mount St. Helens was a truncated dwarf of its former imposing presence. Much of the area to the north and east of Mount St. Helens looked like a moonscape, stripped of vegetation and covered with ash.

Scientists have tried to calculate the number of megatons of energy it would take to lift a cubic mile of mountain 60,000 feet in the air and turn it into burned sulfur and ash—the kind of stuff referred to as brimstone. It is almost impossible to understand the amount of power it would take to produce that cataclysmic event.

In all that happened during that tragic sequence of events, one of the most amazing things to me was the reaction of the reluctant residents when they were warned of the danger and urged to evacuate. Some people heeded the warning, and their lives were spared. Some did not heed the warning, and they paid for it with their lives.

With that thought in mind, let me share something seemingly unrelated but with powerful parallels to Mount St. Helens. We live in a world far different from the one that existed only a few years ago. It seems as though more and more people have lost the compass that had guided them previously. I'm talking about the basic assumptions and deeply held inner values that were at the foundation of society throughout the ages. I'm talking about fundamental values such as respect for human life and for each other, and the necessity of cooperating and working together harmoniously for the common good.

Because of the increasing tendencies toward selfishness, survival-of-the-fittest and might-makes-right attitudes, loss of reverence for human life, and the obsession with self-gratification, our world seems to be experiencing a Mount St. Helens bulge that could blow up with catastrophic results at any time.

The bedrock human values and assumptions in existence at the dawn of civilization formed the foundation from which humankind drew its best instincts and produced its greatest accomplishments. Those bedrock values exist deep within every member of the human race, and when any one of us truly gets in touch with those values, we find fulfillment in life—fulfillment that transcends the baser motivations sometimes exhibited by humankind.

In saying this, I want to emphasize my conviction that all of us have the ability to do just that—to find greater meaning in life and the fulfillment we all hunger for. We have to get in touch with our most deeply held inner values and live our lives consistent with what matters most.

That is one reason I am impelled to write this book. As a people and a civilization we are capable of thinking anew and acting anew if we can get in touch with the basic assumptions and deeply held inner values we share with every other person on this planet.

There is another reason I am writing this book, one that relates more clearly to each of us individually and that we can get our arms around at a personal level. We won't be able to do much about identifying and doing something about the values by which we live collectively as a civilization if we don't first identify and do something about those values that are most important to us as individuals and families. Just as a journey of a thousand miles is undertaken one step at a time, so the healing of our civilization must take place one individual and one family at a time.

I don't have the political clout and wisdom to do much about producing the worldwide cultural sea changes that must happen in order to return civilization to its foundation of shared human values. But I do know something about how to help individuals and families do that, how to help them identify their deeply held governing values—what matters most to them—and then put those values to work in their lives.

So while the values crisis is a worldwide one, this book will deal with solutions on an individual and family level. It outlines a process that will put you in touch with what really matters most to you. By following that process you will come to know yourself better than you have ever known yourself before. The process is based on natural laws, fundamental principles that have governed personal fulfillment and success for thousands of years.

What This Book Can Do for You

In working with and speaking to people all over the world, I have found one concern that seems to be shared by many who talk with me. Almost all express the feeling that life is not the way they wish it to be. They long for something more. Many are people who have achieved great success in their field, but they still talk about a hunger for something more, something deeper and more fulfilling. I hear such comments as:

> Looking at my life, I can't help but feel that some things are seriously amiss. I am troubled by personal problems I've had for years, excess emotional baggage just hanging around that I can't bury or hide or get rid of. I've looked to others for my answers, and I'm just not getting any. What's keeping me from finding the answers?

> I've accomplished just about everything there is to do in my profession, but in the process it has cost me my personal and family life. My marriage is in tatters, and my children don't even know me and I don't really know them anymore. I should be happy, but something's terribly wrong with everything.

I had hoped that technology would help me get more in control, but it has only made it worse! There are more phone messages waiting to be answered, cell phone calls wherever I am, faxes piling up, and emails accumulating. I can't seem to come to grips with all the data. Is this all I can expect from life in the information age?

I really value my health, yet I struggle with my weight and eating right. I've promised myself countless times that I'll get better, but I'm losing hope that I'll ever be able to match my lifestyle with my values.

As the principal owner and CEO of a small business, I love my work and want our company to be known for its contributions. But my coworkers talk behind my back and misinterpret my actions. I feel as though I'm being sabotaged. I have these inner feelings that our company really could make a difference, but I'm having a hard time communicating any of that to others. How can I better define what is really important to me about the company, and then how can I more effectively communicate that to my colleagues? Help!

I'm twenty-one years old, with my life out ahead of me. With my family pushing me one way in terms of career and friends saying that other directions are the way I should go, who has the right answers? Frankly, none of the ideas others are pushing me to pursue appeal to me, but I don't have any better answers. What am I really all about anyway?

It's important to me to be organized, yet my desk and filing system are out of whack. I spend more time shuffling papers looking for things than actually doing the work. Other people seem to be able to get themselves organized, and some don't even worry about a messy work space and still get more done than I do. Why is order so important to me, and why can't I make it happen in my own life?

Do any of those comments seem familiar to you? What they represent is an inner conflict about values, at the personal level rather than the global one. Each of those statements expresses the pain the person was experiencing that comes from losing touch with things that matter the most.

In the rush and press of modern life, too many have lost contact with the deeply held values that matter, such as close family relationships, fulfilling work, giving of self in service to others, following one's own inner light, and sharing time and feelings and dreams with those we care about. Helping you identify those deeply held values and then doing something about them in meaningful everyday living is what this book is all about.

Discovering what really matters most to you won't necessarily be easy. You'll have to do some digging and expend some mental effort to identify what makes you tick. But if you make the effort, you'll discover what lies at the center of your being and you'll be prepared to turn what matters most to you into meaningful goals. Then you can put those deeply held values and goals to work in your daily life. And you will find that you are able to contribute to the larger task of helping your nation and the world community put the most fundamental and shared values to work in the daily life of the planet.

If you follow the process that this book outlines, I can promise you two things: First, that you will come to experience the inner peace that comes from living by your own inner compass. Second, you will unleash inner power and potential you may not realize are there to help you accomplish the things that are most important to you and to the larger communities of which you are a part.

The process will help you understand who you really are—a unique individual with your own mix of talents, aptitudes, strengths, weaknesses, feelings, potentials, and possibilities. In doing this we'll look at all the various *roles* you have in your life—mother, father, partner, son, daughter, provider, nurturer, leader, employee, mentor, student, and others. For each of those roles as well as your life in general we'll identify the inner *governing values* you subscribe to, values that govern how you live and function in those roles. From those roles and governing values you will then define your own *Personal Mission Statement* that concisely states your purpose in life.

Be aware that there are no right or wrong answers, only *your* answers. The goal is to find out what matters most to you, not what others think should matter most to you.

As we do this, you will come to see the synergy and power that arises naturally from seeing these interrelationships clearly—your roles, your governing values, and your sense of personal mission, the three fundamental elements that define who you really are and what matters most to you.

Once you have created a clear picture of the real you, we'll move to the remaining steps of the process. I'll show you how to identify meaningful long-range goals related to the roles you have and the governing values associated with them. Then we'll look at ways to make sure you are doing something about accomplishing those goals on a daily basis, for when your daily actions reflect and relate to what matters most to you, you will experience the greatest of all prizes: inner peace. To help you in your efforts to change unwanted behavior, we'll take a look at how your beliefs—what you perceive to be true about life and the world in which you live—can either distort or more clearly focus your efforts depending on how closely those beliefs reflect reality.

We will also touch upon how the process can be applied to business and how the principles behind the process have been at the heart of the lives and work of key individuals throughout history who have brought about pivotal change and many of the major turning points in the march of the human experience. Finally, I'll add some of my own thoughts on what this process has meant in my life.

What's in the Rest of the Book?

The book contains four parts, each with several chapters.

Part One talks about the power of knowing who you are. First, we will look at people who seem to know who they are, who "have it together," and the power that comes from this kind of self-knowledge. Many of the "heroes" in our lives, those individuals we look up to and desire to emulate, seem to have that quality. In chapter 1 we'll identify some of the common patterns among these kinds of people to see what they can teach us about our own personal quests to know who we are.

In chapter 2 we discuss "life overload," a challenge common to the age in which we live. We'll look at the many pressures and factors that prevent us from examining what matters most to us and keep us from doing something about them. When you are aware of those pressures and their effects, you will be better prepared to deal with them proactively and effectively.

Chapter 3 deals with a yearning common to almost all people—"Someday I'm going to . . ." You'll learn about the importance of having and doing something about those yearnings and how they are an important key to identifying what matters most to you. We'll also talk about making and breaking New Year's resolutions and the pain that comes when a major gap exists between our dreams and what we do about them.

Part Two, the heart of the book, will help you get down to the business of discovering what matters most to you. You'll learn about the "tri-quation" of roles, values, and mission, and the relationships among these fundamental elements in discovering who you are and, consequently, what matters most to you.

Chapter 4 will help you look at yourself as a unique individual and the roles you play in your life. In chapter 5 we'll take a closer look at what governing values are, how they influence our behavior, and how our actions are generally consistent with our deeply held values. We'll examine where governing values come from and, via a series of simple but enlightening exercises, help you identify and refine your own personal list. Then I'll show you how to prioritize your values and write clarifying statements stating what each one means to you.

Chapter 6 will show you how to identify and put in writing your personal mission, your larger purpose in life as it relates to the roles and values you have defined. That done, you will have created a clear and concise statement of who you are.

Chapter 7 brings your roles, governing values, and personal mission back together to help you understand the power that grows from the synergistic relationship among these three aspects of what matters most to you.

In Part Three we move into actually doing something about what matters most to you. In chapter 8 we'll talk about the importance of planning, of premeditating a course of action, and I'll help you establish specific time-dimensioned and measurable goals. Chapter 9 will teach you how to translate those goals into intermediate steps and daily tasks.

We'll also talk about how to overcome the obstacles that keep you from achieving your value-related goals. These obstacles range from worrying about what people will think to secret doubts, fear of change, and the walls we sometimes build around ourselves. You'll find practical help in dealing with these obstacles. Chapter 10 will help you see what is written on your personal "Belief Window," how to find out if your beliefs are congruent with reality, and how what you believe is real can hinder or help you live in concert with what matters most to you.

Part Four looks at the broader view of the process. Chapter 11 discusses how organizations and even governments are unique in the same sense that people are. They have their own sets of roles and values that govern how they function as an organization and in their marketplace or environment. They also have a purpose or mission, and the best of them have identified that mission. As with people, the process of consciously identifying organizational roles, governing values, and mission unleashes a power and focus that can be the difference between success and failure.

Chapter 12 shifts to the global view. We'll look at how the power of one individual with a life firmly rooted in inner values and motivated by a powerful sense of mission can literally change the world.

In chapter 13 we'll look at how roles, values, and missions can change over a lifetime and the need to keep ourselves from getting too rigid or set in our ways. As Lincoln so powerfully taught, our circumstances will change, and we, too, must be able to change and react to change. Chapter 14 provides insight into something I call the "Abundance Mentality," an other-centered approach to living that is often the result of being in touch with what matters most in your life.

In a concluding chapter, you are provided with some reinforcement for the idea that you really can do it. You really can live in line with what matters most to you on a daily basis. You'll see how others have done it, and they'll share with you how they overcame obstacles and tell you about the rewards of their efforts.

"Be Yourself, but Be That Perfectly"

While grappling with and teaching these concepts over the years, I have gained a deeper appreciation of the vital role that governing values play in our lives. I also understand more clearly that our governing values lie close to the heart of who we are, in that part of our being which defines each of us as unique and special. I have seen how the process of discovering who we really are unlocks an inner power, a driving force that can aid us in our personal quest to do something about the things that matter most to us. And I have experienced, through personal difficulties in my marriage and family relationships, the very real pain that comes when we act in opposition to our deeply held values.

This book is written with both hope and a degree of anguish. The anguish comes from the pain of experiences that have powerfully demonstrated to me the need to have our daily actions in line with what we hold most important in our lives. But the hope arises from the personal reaffirmations about the healing power that comes from knowing who we are and living in harmony with what we know matters most to us.

I also hope that the insights I have gained will benefit others. I have seen how the natural laws behind this process work in my own life and in the lives of others. I have shared these concepts in seminars and speeches across America and elsewhere in the world, and I have been gratified by the responses. I am sure they will be beneficial and helpful in your life quest.

A great leader who was influential in shaping my life once said, "Be yourself, but be that perfectly." What a wonderful thought! What a powerful affirmation of the potential and power that lies within each of us! When you have finished this book, I'm confident that you will know yourself better and find yourself on the road to being yourself—more perfectly.

Part One

The Power
of Knowing Who
You Are

Wherever you go, go with all your heart.

Confucius

SEVERAL years ago an American writer and scientist named Michael Hart wrote a book entitled *The 100: A Ranking of the Most Influential Persons in History,* an attempt to rank the one hundred people who have had the most impact on the world, along with a capsule biography of each.

The book aroused a good deal of controversy, principally over who was included and who was not, and the order in which they were ranked. Hart put Muhammad at the top of his list, followed by Sir Isaac Newton, Jesus Christ, and Buddha. No American was listed among the top ten; in fact, the highest-ranked American was George Washington, at twenty-six, behind several names that most Americans would not even recognize. Benjamin Franklin and Abraham Lincoln were not even in the top one hundred; they made honorable mention.

Hart's top choices have not been universally applauded, but the author makes a spirited and reasoned defense of his choices in the foreword. He says they were made in terms of numbers of people impacted and the effects of that impact over time. He points out that Muhammad's direct influence and precepts rapidly spread across a vast part of the world, from western Africa to the islands of Indonesia, dramatically transforming the cultures they encountered. These strong religious and secular influences have continued over thirteen centuries and remain a potent force today.

Likewise, Hart notes that Newton, as the father of modern science, has had a tremendous impact on the way the world lives today. The scientific revolution he began radically transformed politics, economics, communication, transportation, agriculture, medicine, and just about every other aspect of life. Our world would be completely different without the scientific knowledge and technology that Newton's discoveries set in motion.

Hart also points out that Jesus' impact, especially on the development of European civilization and its later extension to the New World, has also been dramatic, while the teachings of Buddha profoundly impacted the diverse cultures in India and east Asia. The influence of each of the top four on Hart's list outlasted their lifetimes and has even grown dramatically.

The book makes fascinating reading not only because of the way these historical figures were ranked by the author but because it provides glimpses of who these individuals were and the contributions they made. I won't wade into the debate on who was the most important or influential, but I am impressed that most of these people almost inevitably had a strong sense of identity. They knew who they were, and that knowledge invariably gave them power that helped them accomplish what mattered most to them in their lives.

In chapter 1 we will look at heroes, those who strongly influence us, bring out the best in us, and inspire us to be more than we are.

We'll look at the sources of inner power they seem to have, examine some of the common characteristics they exhibit, and see what lessons we can learn from them.

The daunting thing about heroes is that they may cause us to think, "I could never do what they do. I can't get it together the way they can." Part of this is a reflection of the time in which we live, and chapter 2 will examine life in the age of gridlock. We'll explore some of the reasons we don't always live up to our own desires and expectations, and we'll take issue with some of the myths about our ability to overcome the hectic nature of modern life and focus on things that are really important to us.

Then in chapter 3 we will start to move toward the heart of the book. We will talk about our desires to accomplish our dreams and find real fulfillment in life someday.

But that's getting ahead of the story. It is time now to take a look at our heroes.

Chapter 1

Heroes: People Who Know Who They Are

There is no chance, no fate, no destiny that can circumvent, or hinder, or control a firm resolve of a determined soul.

—*Ella Wheeler Wilcox*

It has been said that we live in an age when there are no heroes. I strongly disagree. While teaching and speaking with people about how to find and live by their deeply held values, I have heard about many heroes who have been role models and sources of inspiration for people both famous and obscure.

If I were to ask you to make a list of the heroes in your life, you would probably come up with several people you admire who have had an impact on your personal or professional life. There have been many such heroes for me, individuals for whom I have immense love and respect, who have brought out the best in me, and whose lives or characteristics have inspired me to find out who I really am.

Winston Churchill and England's Darkest Hour

Perhaps my reasons for talking about heroes can best be illustrated by referring to one of my own sources of inspiration, Winston Churchill. He has been one of my heroes since high school when another hero, a high school teacher (more about him later), first awakened my interest in history and I became aware of Churchill's vital role in the outcome of World War II. In recent years I have been taken aback to learn that many of those who have grown up since World War II know so little about him. He appears to be just a name if he shows up on their radar scopes at all, whereas I believe Winston Churchill's actions were pivotal in one of the great and most dramatic turning points of civilization.

We must start with the fact that the future did not look at all promising for England's survival in May 1940 when Churchill became its prime minister. A little more than twenty years had passed since Britain and her allies had defeated Germany in what was widely considered "the war to end all wars." But now the reborn military might of Adolf Hitler's Nazi Germany was overrunning Holland and Belgium and pushing into France in what seemed to be a crushing replay of the opening of the earlier war. This time the German blitzkrieg appeared to be unstoppable.

For most of the previous five years Hitler had thumbed his nose at the world community, rearming his nation and reoccupying former German territory given to France after World War I. He had engineered the German annexation of Austria in a bloodless coup. In the so-called Munich accords in the fall of 1938, Hitler had used deceit to persuade England's Prime Minister Neville Chamberlain and France's Premier Edouard Daladier to give in to his demands to occupy and "protect" the German-speaking portions of Czechoslovakia. That done, Hitler promptly gobbled up the rest of the country less than six months later. Only late in this period had the British begun to rearm themselves, and they were seriously outnumbered in terms of men in uniform and modern military equipment. They could only hope that France's strong army would be able to deter further German moves.

In September 1939, Hitler's armies entered Poland, in direct defiance of the promises he had made at Munich. The British and French, having promised to aid Poland if it was attacked, reluctantly declared war on Germany. It was a case of too little, too late because within weeks Hitler subdued and occupied Poland.

In May 1940, after a winter in which the armies of Germany and France faced each other across the fortifications of France's supposedly impregnable Maginot Line, Hitler appeared to be unstoppable again. Wheeling through the Low Countries, the German tanks simply outflanked the French border fortresses, and they appeared capable of quickly reaching Paris.

The proclamation of "peace for our time" with which Chamberlain had originally hailed the Munich agreement with Hitler had turned out to be anything but. On May 9 the now discredited Chamberlain resigned, recommending to King George VI that Winston Churchill be named his successor.

Although Churchill was a member of Chamberlain's Conservative Party, he had been one of the leading critics of Chamberlain and of the party's handling of the entire German situation. Following Munich, Churchill had declared that the prime minister's "peace for our time" was "an unmitigated disaster." A weary Chamberlain was now saying in effect, "I've failed. You see if you can do any better." On May 10, Winston Churchill was summoned to Buckingham Palace. In his words: "Presently a message arrived summoning me to the Palace at six o'clock. . . . I was taken immediately to the King. His Majesty received me most graciously and bade me sit down. He looked at me searchingly and quizzically for some moments, and then said: '. . . I want to ask you to form a Government.' I said I would certainly do so."

Following his appointment, Churchill met with political and military leaders, advisers, and others, and they put together a coalition government. This was happening while the roar and clash of battle continued on the Continent.

Someone in Winston Churchill's position at that time might have felt some misgivings about the menace his nation faced. He might have felt the oppressive burden of leadership during those perilous times and perhaps some apprehension about his ability to change events. Not so, as revealed in his memoirs:

> As I went to bed at about 3 A.M., I was conscious of a profound sense of relief. At last I had the authority to give directions over the whole scene. I felt as if I were walking with Destiny, and that all my past life had been but a preparation for this hour and for this trial. . . . My warnings over the last six years had been so numerous, so detailed, and were now so terribly vindicated, that no one could gainsay me. I could not be reproached either

for making the war or with want of preparation for it. I thought I knew a good deal about it all, and I was sure I should not fail. Therefore, although impatient for the morning, I slept soundly and had no need for cheering dreams. Facts are better than dreams.

Reading these words, I feel a great surge of emotion. Churchill was a man who was in the right place at the right time, and as a result he made a powerful difference for the entire world—a difference that certainly puts him on anyone's list as one of the most influential persons of the twentieth century.

At 3 o'clock on the morning of May 11, 1940, Winston Churchill clearly seemed to be a man who "had it all together," who knew who he was and what he was capable of doing in the crisis he faced. Let's look at what his words reveal about the man at this critical time.

After being asked by his king to form a new government, he works long into the night to put together a government in the midst of chaos and despair. Finally, as he goes to bed, he is "conscious of a profound sense of relief."

Relief? He was taking over the leadership of an unprepared country that was at war with the greatest military machine that had ever been created up to that point in history. Having just been given the biggest task of his life, he was experiencing "relief." He was having feelings of calmness and serenity. How could he possibly feel that upbeat, given the circumstances?

Churchill provides his own answer to that question: "At last I had the authority to give directions over the whole scene. I felt as if I were walking with Destiny." Have you ever felt that you had authority over the whole scene of your personal life? Have you ever felt that you were walking with destiny in your life? Winston Churchill did, and his words reveal a quiet confidence, a sense of self-worth. He was certain about his ability to lead and to find the answers that would bring his people through the crisis.

You're probably thinking, "That's all fine, but I'm not a Winston Churchill." Yet I believe we are all capable of having those same feelings of confidence and self-worth about our own spheres of influence. We may not have to face a crisis that involves saving the world, as Churchill did, but whatever our challenges in life may be, we are each capable of gaining the same kind of sureness and confidence.

We are going to talk about how to do just that. When you finally decide to take control of your life, to identify what matters most to you, to choose a direction and plan so that you know exactly where you're going and how to get there, you will have the same sense of relief that Churchill described in the midst of his country's darkest hour.

Winston Churchill's words also tell us something about how he arrived at this point: "all my past life had been but a preparation for this hour and for this trial." Churchill's earlier political life had not been a bed of roses. He had even been out of favor in his own party as much as he had been in. But as he ascended to the pinnacle of political prominence, he seemed to realize that, in the words of General George C. Marshall who would head the U.S. Army during World War II, no defeat is ever final, it is just preparation for the next and greater battle.

So here was Winston Churchill, recognizing that he was prepared to take on this magnificent challenge, and as he reflected on his new responsibility, other things went through his mind. "I could not be reproached either for making the war or with want of preparation for it. I thought I knew a great deal about it all, *and I was sure I should not fail*" (emphasis added).

Churchill wasn't going into this ignorant of the facts. He had been thinking about and preparing for it for much of the previous six years. He had evaluated the situation, had carefully studied what he could of Hitler's war-making capability, and knew the strength and power of the British people when backed up against the wall. He knew that if he could rally the mind, spirit, and heart of the British people, they would eventually emerge victorious. On the eve of what could have been a disaster, Winston Churchill was able to say, "I was sure I should not fail." I stand in awe of the confidence that statement proclaims.

I also love the final lines of that quotation from his war memoirs: "Therefore, although impatient for the morning, I slept soundly and had no need for cheering dreams. Facts are better than dreams." Here Churchill exhibits what I have heard called a "divine impatience for the sun to come up the next morning." He couldn't wait to get started. He must have had some sense of the enormous task ahead. He knew all too well the state of the forces at his disposal and the resources needed to make it happen. He knew other allies needed to be involved in the effort, including a reluctant, isolationist United States. And still he couldn't wait for the next morning.

Have you ever found yourself impatient for the sun to come up? People without vision have no interest in seeing the sun come up the next day. But people *with* vision experience what Churchill experienced. They can't wait, and as soon as that sun comes up, they are out of bed. They have energy. They have excitement. They have a plan. They have vision. They know exactly where they are going and how they are going to get there.

So what happened after that fateful day in early May 1940? Armed with little more than the power of knowing who he was, Churchill first rallied a downcast and fearful nation with some of the most ringing oratory the world has ever heard. On June 4, 1940, less than a month after becoming prime minister, Churchill rose in the House of Commons to report on the progress of the war. The outlook was not good. The French were on the verge of collapse, about to surrender to Nazi Germany. The British had just about been able to evacuate from France much of their expeditionary force, which had been surrounded by the Germans at the northern French port of Dunkirk, but they had been forced to leave much military equipment behind. They now faced the almost certain invasion of their own island. In this deepening crisis, Winston Churchill outlined the situation to the House of Commons and closed with these stirring words:

> We shall go on to the end, we shall fight in France, we shall fight on the seas and oceans, we shall fight with growing confidence and growing strength in the air, we shall defend our Island, whatever the cost may be, we shall fight on the beaches, we shall fight on the landing grounds, we shall fight in the fields and in the streets, we shall fight in the hills; we shall never surrender, and even if, which I do not for a moment believe, this Island or a large part of it were subjugated and starving, then our Em-

pire beyond the seas, armed and guarded by the British Fleet, would carry on the struggle, until, in God's good time, the New World, with all its power and might, steps forth to the rescue and the liberation of the old.

It took another year and a half before the United States entered the war and tipped the balance in favor of Great Britain and her allies. In all that time, during which German aerial bombardment destroyed large sections of London and many British industrial cities, and citizens were armed with pitchforks and ancient firearms as they prepared to defend themselves against invasion, Churchill continued to thunder defiance at Hitler and marshaled what meager resources he had to fight back. During those months, Winston Churchill not only saved Britain from defeat but, understood now in retrospect, he saved democracy as a form of government in the world. Here was truly a single individual whose life made a profound difference to everyone on our planet.

Other Heroes, Extraordinary and Ordinary

In thinking about my own heroes and talking with others about heroes, I am aware that they do not have to be Winston Churchills or other great historical figures. Some heroes are found in today's sports and media culture, some in unlikely places with unlikely missions. But most are ordinary individuals who know who they are and have discovered the power that comes from that special knowledge. Let's look at three such people; two are well known to almost everyone in the world, and the other is known to a relative few and probably doesn't realize that he is a hero. But he is a big hero to me.

Michael Jordan

In our age of instantaneous communication and widespread interest in sports, is there anyone on earth who has not heard of Michael Jordan? When he retired from the National Basketball Association in 1998, he was considered by many the best player ever to have played the game. This verdict came not only from his peers but from almost anyone who understands the game of basketball. There aren't many people who have received such recognition in the professional basketball arena.

There is no question that Michael Jordan was blessed with the physical equipment to be a great athlete. You couldn't watch him play and not immediately be aware that he has a marvelous body for the sport. He has huge hands that handle a basketball much like an orange. He is extremely well proportioned, very muscular, and is a picture-perfect athletic specimen. But many athletes with similar equipment and physical attributes have not come close to accomplishing what Michael Jordan did.

Why was he so much better than everyone else? We talked about Winston Churchill and his magnificent preparation for the role he played in saving the world. We talked about some of the basic attributes or evidences when someone has it all together. Michael Jordan is one of those people, I believe, who has it all together.

I followed Michael Jordan's career peripherally until the 1996–97 and 1997–98 seasons when the Utah Jazz were pitted against the Chicago Bulls in the NBA championships. Being from Utah, I've naturally been a Jazz fan for quite a few years. I got to know many of the players on the team between 1986 and 1989 when I accompanied the Jazz team as they traveled to many high schools throughout the state as part of an antidrug campaign. I have great respect for John Stockton, Karl Malone, and the other excellent athletes on the Utah Jazz team, but in both of those championships the Bulls were absolutely unbeatable—in large part because of Michael Jordan.

During game six of the 1998 championship series, I came to understand the magnificence of Michael Jordan. The five previous games had been very difficult for both teams. The Jazz had narrowly won game five in Chicago to bring the series back to Utah. Chicago led the series three games to two. With forty-three seconds left in the game, Utah was ahead. With about five seconds left, the Jazz were one point ahead. All Karl Malone had to do was hold on to the ball, and we would have won game six, taking the series to a seventh and final game. Then Michael Jordan, in a flashing, split-second, magnificently beautiful athletic move, stole the ball from Karl Malone when he relaxed for a nanosecond—just long enough for

Jordan to make the steal. Jordan then raced down the court, out-foxed Bryon Russell, scored the basket, won the game, and won the series. It was all over. The Chicago Bulls returned to Chicago with their sixth world championship.

Part of the miracle of television is the magnificent coverage given these athletic events. Viewers are able to see activity that could not be seen from the fiftieth row of the Delta Center in Salt Lake City. I wish I could somehow show you the television image of Michael Jordan's face as he moved in on Karl Malone to steal that ball. The fire and determination in his eyes was awe-inspiring. You couldn't watch Michael Jordan play basketball without noticing his intensity, his immense desire to play well and to win. And that desire motivated him to do things that people when they talk or write about his prowess still can't believe occurred. Like Winston Churchill, Michael Jordan is a person who has exhibited the quality of having it all together, of knowing exactly who he is and where he wants to go. That, in my opinion, is why Michael Jordan is a hero to so many and is respected—even by his fiercest opponents.

Mother Teresa, the Little Nun Who Became a Household Name Worldwide

Most people today have probably heard about Mother Teresa of Calcutta, India, who died in 1997 after a lifetime of service to the poor and needy. Who was this diminutive woman who probably didn't weigh 110 pounds ever in her life, and why did she have such an impact on the world? What is it about her which created such love and respect that she appears likely for eventual sainthood in the Roman Catholic Church?

If you put Mother Teresa's talents and skills into the profile of the typical success pattern that modern society seems to look for, she doesn't qualify for the kind of universal acclaim and notoriety that she had. She was born in humble circumstances in Skopje, Macedonia, part of the former Yugoslavia. She wasn't highly educated. She did not have the charisma that often comes with being large in stature. She had very few "marketable skills" of the kind that the world seems to think are essential for influence and success today.

What was it about her, then, that promoted her into the white lights of acclaim on a world stage?

The answer is simple and yet very powerful. It is all wrapped up in a word and concept called *service*. At the age of eighteen she entered a convent in Ireland, and from that time on she dedicated her life to serving her fellow human beings. In 1929 she arrived in Calcutta and began to teach in a school for girls. The misery and affliction of the masses of people in India greatly touched her, and over the next several years her compassion moved her to try to ease their pain and suffering.

On September 10, 1946, on a long train ride to Darjeeling, India, where she was traveling to recover from suspected tuberculosis, Mother Teresa had a life-changing spiritual experience: "I realized that I had the call to take care of the sick and the dying, the hungry, the naked, the homeless—to be God's love in action to the poorest of the poor. That was the beginning of the Missionaries of Charity."

At this point Mother Teresa took this mission most seriously. She didn't just try to do more to help those in need, she went right to the top of her church and asked permission to leave the religious order to which she belonged and establish a new order of sisters. After receiving that permission from Pope Pius XII, she went to work in Calcutta, long known as having one of the worst concentrations of human misery in the world. She spent the rest of her days trying to ease their physical and spiritual suffering. From the legacy Mother Teresa has left us, we can see the familiar pattern common to many heroes: She knew exactly who she was, what was most important to her, what she was about, and what she wanted to accomplish on this earth.

One of the amazing aspects of Mother Teresa's story is how she stood out in a quest that many have been motivated to do. There are great stories of nurses, missionaries, humanitarians, and others who have done marvelous things in serving those less fortunate. Why was Mother Teresa singled out as an icon of this concept? The answer to that seems quite simple to me as well. It is wrapped up in a word and concept called *consistency*. Mother Teresa consistently went about living her life in accordance with the mission she had identified for herself. She clearly wasn't in it for the personal accolades that it ultimately brought. She was in it because she wanted to bring hope and peace, and end the suffering of people who were sick and dying in the streets of Calcutta.

I have never been to Calcutta, but I've heard from those who have been there that nowhere else in the world has the poverty, sickness, and filth you'll find there. But this is where Mother Teresa decided she was going to make a difference. The statistics show that over the years more than forty-two thousand people were treated at an abandoned Hindu temple that she was able to acquire and convert into the Kalighat Home for the Dying. The nuns would go out and literally take from the streets of Calcutta those who were sick and dying and bring them to the home, where they received love and kindness. To many it would seem like a hopeless and thankless task. More than nineteen thousand died there, but at least they died in a place where people were caring for and loving them.

Mother Teresa's story gradually became known to the world. People were stunned by this inspiring departure from the usual prevalent attitude of "it's terrible, but I can't do anything about it." People simply couldn't comprehend this little dynamo who had created her own order of sisters to help the sick, dying, and needy. As a result, she had a tremendous impact on the world. Perhaps the reason the world has heard of this woman who labored in a faraway place is that she lived her life with a deep understanding of what mattered most, a commitment to doing something about those things, and a willingness to sacrifice the energy of her life for and on behalf of the people to whom she had dedicated it.

Robert Niederholzer

As I look back and seriously reflect on those who personally impacted me in life-changing ways, one of the major players was Robert Niederholzer. I grew up in the Hawaiian Islands. My father and mother moved our family there in 1946 when I was two years old. My father had accepted the chairmanship of the speech department at the University of Hawaii. The plan was to spend two years in Hawaii and then return to the University of Utah where my father had his residency. Our family liked Hawaii so well that we ended up staying thirty years, so I spent my early years, up through high school, in Honolulu.

When I was a junior in high school, my father accepted an exchange teaching job with a teacher from New York University. He swapped jobs and homes for one year as a cross-pollination effort on the part of both institutions for two of their senior professors. So I got to spend my junior year of high school in Douglaston, Long Island, and attended Bayside High School. If you want an interesting experience in culture shock, you ought to move from a small high school in Honolulu to a major public high school in New York City—300 kids in Hawaii, 4,500 kids in New York. It was an amazing experience. When I returned to Hawaii for my senior year, my homeroom teacher turned out to be a new addition to the faculty—not a local person from the islands but a man from the mainland, Robert Niederholzer.

Like many in the class, I was upset that our homeroom teacher for our last year in high school was an outsider, and not even a local person but somebody from the mainland. How awful! It didn't take us long to recognize, however, that Robert Niederholzer was a very different kind of teacher. Up to my senior year, being successful scholastically was not one of my long suits. If I maintained a C average in my classes, I was delighted. I was interested in lots of other stuff besides homework, exams, and the kinds of things that should be focused on when you're in high school. Instead, I was very involved in athletics and participated in basketball, softball, swimming, tennis, and some track events. I was also very much involved in high school politics as senior class president, and so the "school" part of school was just sort of a hindrance to me.

I had never been much of a reader until my senior year in high school. I didn't enjoy reading; I was slow at it and so didn't do much of it. Mr. Niederholzer changed all that. For the first time in my life I found myself discovering the magic of learning from books. It started with his insisting that I read the first volume of Bruce Catton's classic trilogy *The History of the Civil War.* This is where my fascination with the Civil War began. I fell in love with that period of American history and in later years found myself, whenever I could, visiting battlefields all over the South and central Northeast looking for the sites where those amazing events took place.

It was interesting to me how Mr. Niederholzer did it. It wasn't a matter of his saying, "Gee, I think you ought to read this book, Hyrum." It was, "You *will* read this book. You have five days." It was something he insisted on. Initially, out of fear, I would start the books, but by the time I was into the second or third chapter, I was hooked. I think he knew I would be hooked and would get the assignments done. When one book was finished, he immediately had one following it. I probably read more books that year than in all previous years of my schooling put together.

During that time a statement my father had made when I was much younger started to make sense to me. He said, "You cannot think any deeper than your vocabulary will allow you to." As I read the books for Mr. Niederholzer's class, I realized that the best way to build a vocabulary is to read. When you discover a word you don't understand, look up its meaning so you will know what the author is trying to say. I found myself doing that, and my vocabulary started to build. (Speaking of vocabularies, I have heard it said that Winston Churchill had one of the largest vocabularies of anybody alive. And recent studies seem to indicate that a large vocabulary is one of the common denominators of truly successful people.)

Robert Niederholzer was by no means a conventional kind of teacher. There were times that year when I got angry at the pressure he was putting on me. There were times when I thought there was no way I would get everything read. He seemed to sense what my capacity was and never stretched me further than I could endure, but he was always there, insisting and pushing and driving and demanding that I perform.

It's interesting to look back on an experience like that. Now I have this intense appreciation for this man for caring enough to push me the way he did. In retrospect I realize that he really did love me and the rest of the kids in that class. You could tell that by what he was willing to do for and with us. It wasn't just a seven-hour-a-day job for him. He was on the phone with us, he was in our homes; we were in his home, we went on retreats together. He did everything he could to introduce us to the power of our minds. As Kahlil Gibran said in his book of poetry, *The Prophet*, "A great teacher does not lead you to the threshold of his or her knowledge but leads you to the threshold of your own mind." Robert Niederholzer was a master at doing that, and as a result of his passion and dedication, my life changed dramatically for the good in my senior year of high school.

As I look back now, Robert Niederholzer knew who he was and what he should be doing. In the process, he helped me and a lot of others discover something of who we were and what we could be doing.

A Profile of Those Who "Have It Together"

In looking at the lives of personal heroes, I want to emphasize that I am not talking about heroes strictly as role models. For example, Michael Jordan has been an inspiration and role model for many aspiring young basketball players, but you could spend a lot of frustrated and fruitless time trying to play basketball like Michael Jordan because you can't be Michael Jordan. The same goes for anyone we look up to and would like to emulate. The role of heroes in our lives doesn't work that way. The true role of heroes is to inspire us to be the best we are capable of being. In the well-known phrase from the U. S. Army enlistment commercials, "Be all that you can be."

Some of the most helpful things our heroes can demonstrate for us are the patterns characteristic of people who are "all that they can be." If we look at their lives and behavior, several such patterns begin to emerge. One overall pattern is that they achieve success in their lives. I don't mean success in the materialistic, monetary way it has come to be defined in our day. I mean success in terms of living in harmony with the good things deep within us and uniquely ours. In the introduction to this book I mentioned the leader who impacted my late teenage years and said, "Be yourself, but be that perfectly." To me all the heroes we've talked about did just that. They were and are themselves as perfect as they were capable of being.

Reflect on those people you have known who seemed to have it all together. Their success has come as much from who they are as from what they accomplished. They're generally optimistic, they exhibit an inner peace, and most often they succeed at what they try to accomplish—mentally, emotionally, spiritually, and temporally. Not every one of them will exhibit all the characteristics we've been talking about, but there are some basic ones that apply to most of them. Let's look at some of the patterns common among people who "have it together":

SELF-AWARENESS. These people know who they are. They know their abilities and strengths, what they are capable of doing, and how to accomplish it. With the power that flows from such knowledge, they are capable of accomplishing the impossible even when physically small or frail (like Mother Teresa).

CONFIDENCE. They lack fear. Winston Churchill knew deep inside that he would not fail. Perhaps more than anything else, that confidence carried him and the people of Britain through that terrible trial in their history.

SELF-WORTH. This is most often evidenced in their focus, not on themselves but on those they serve and work with. We saw this evidenced by Mother Teresa and my tough but loving high school teacher, Mr. Niederholzer, who cared enough to light the lamp of learning within me.

A SENSE OF URGENCY. This means a "divine impatience" about everything they do. Winston Churchill impatiently went to bed at 3 o'clock in the morning after having all the burdens of being prime minister placed on him. Such people can't wait for the sun to come up.

A STRONG SENSE OF PERSONAL MISSION. There is a vision of what needs to be done and a passion and focus about doing it. Throughout her lifetime Mother Teresa remained intensely focused on what she felt was a call from God to ease the pain and suffering of the poor.

PERSONAL MAGNETISM. People are drawn to them, and they are able to give "the sure sound of the trumpet." Churchill was able to rally the British people under circumstances that could have made many fail.

AWARENESS AND RESPECT FOR THEIR OWN UNIQUENESS. They don't compare themselves to others or worry about what they're not. Their focus is on what they are.

A CONSISTENCY TO THEIR LIVES. They are not tossed to and fro with every new idea or opportunity or change of events. Like Mother Teresa, some inner sense of consistency keeps them moving toward accomplishing their personal mission in spite of everything that is going on around them.

A SENSE OF CALMNESS AND SERENITY. They are often people who can keep their heads when all about them are losing theirs.

These patterns are not just the exclusive property of the great and successful people of the world. This book is dedicated to the premise that each of us is capable of being ourselves perfectly, of knowing who we are and being able to draw upon the power that comes from that personal and very special knowledge. You are a unique creation, one of a kind, endowed with your own particular mix of talents, abilities, strengths, weaknesses, inner dreams, and potential.

In order to realize who you are, you'll have to be painfully honest with yourself. You may have to set aside a lot of baggage. You may have to deal with others who have good intentions but no right to tell you who or what you should be.

In the process you'll find a sense of purpose that may have been hidden for a long time. You'll also discover a deep and abiding faith in yourself and, more than likely, a strength that comes both from within and, I believe, from spiritual forces beyond yourself. Most of all, you will be able to find the courage to be truly and perfectly YOU.

Chapter 2

"One Hundred Years Ago They Had More Time"

Never live in the past, but always learn from it.

—Anonymous

In the seminars I teach and speeches I give about living more effectively, people often say to me, almost wistfully, "I wish I had lived one hundred years ago when they had more time."

My response to that is "Really? How much more time did they have one hundred years ago than we have now?"

And the response is usually something like "Well . . . they had a whole lot more time."

Reflecting on that widespread desire, I have come to realize that the only difference between now and one hundred years ago is that we have more options in how we use our time than they had a century ago. One of the reasons we have more options is that we can do things faster. With modern household appliances, what took a housewife a week to do one hundred years ago can now be done in three hours on Monday morning. Instead of taking two or three hours to prepare dinner, we can now do it in twenty minutes.

One hundred years ago people had already shortened the time needed to cross North America from three months in a stagecoach or wagon train to less than a week on a train. Today we can go from New York to San Francisco in four and one-half hours, eating dinner and watching a movie as we fly across the continent at more than 600 miles per hour.

The Wagon Train

This contrast in time available to us was forcefully brought home to me in an experience my wife, Gail, and I had in the summer of 1997.

As part of the commemoration of the 150th year after the 1,500-mile trek of the Mormon pioneers from Illinois to Utah in 1846 and 1847, a group of modern-day pioneers decided to reenact the original journey. The objective was to provide an experience that would be typical of journeys made by thousands of American pioneer families and individuals seeking new homes in the Far West or their fortunes in the gold fields of California and elsewhere. The effort attracted considerable attention from American as well as foreign news media; their entourage was almost as big as the wagon train itself.

After leaving Nauvoo, Illinois, and crossing the Mississippi River, it took the original pioneers almost four months to traverse the 350 miles across Iowa. After building a temporary village of log cabins near modern-day Omaha, Nebraska, they spent a harsh winter and made plans to move more than 1,000 miles up the Platte River, across the Rocky Mountains, to the valley of the Great Salt Lake. There they hoped to find a place to live in peace, free of the persecution and misunderstanding that had been their lot in the more settled parts of the eastern United States.

In April 1847 a vanguard company left the encampment on a route that the others would follow. Nearly four months later they arrived at their destination and started what would become Salt Lake City, Utah. Between 1847 and 1869—when the transcontinental railroad was completed with the driving of a golden spike in northern Utah—more than seventy thousand people made that journey in ox- or horse-drawn covered wagons. More than six thousand of them died on the way and were buried along the trail. This migration to the valleys of Utah represented just a fraction of the millions of Americans who followed the trails to new lives in the West during the years before and after the Civil War.

When this group of hardy twentieth-century folks decided to

reenact that trek of 150 years earlier, my wife and I decided to join it for a couple of weeks. We met the wagon train in Jeffery City, a remote town in the high country of Wyoming. Leaving our automobile and horse trailer there, we traveled on horseback with the group for 140 miles. The wagon train covered only about 14 miles per day, so it took us ten days to cross the Continental Divide and travel on to the Green River, all of this through country and terrain that has changed little since the days of those first pioneers. We crossed the same streams, struggled up the same rocky stretches of trail, and gazed at the same distant panorama of mountains and plains. Those ten days were truly a watershed experience for Gail and me. Until then I thought I had a pretty good idea of what those pioneers had gone through, but I discovered that I had absolutely no inkling.

About thirty-five wagons were pulled either by mules or horses, including some big Clydesdales. The wagons were built just like wagons of 150 years ago, and they made a lot of noise. There were also over 150 people pulling or pushing their belongings in two-wheeled handcarts.

At 4 o'clock on our first morning, the wagonmaster began beating on a large steel ring to notify everybody to prepare for that day's journey. We rousted ourselves out of our bedrolls and began the process of moving the wagon train. We had to feed, water, and saddle the horses. We had to prepare breakfast and get everything ready so that the wagon train could move at precisely 7 A.M. We did everything that the original pioneers had done, on the exact day they did it, and we even camped each day at the same spot along the trail where they had camped.

It was exciting to realize that we were in the actual ruts the pioneers had traveled. Each day's journey took about eight or nine hours, and during that time I listened to the clatter of the wagons; saw, smelled, and choked on the dust; watched it cake up on my clothes, saddle, and horse; and realized how dirty everyone was getting. I also saw the bleeding feet of the people who were walking and witnessed a runaway wagon or two. The major cause of death 150 years ago was accidents with large animals. It was sobering to realize that because the pioneers didn't have the facilities or medical technology to care for people, they would bleed to death or get gangrene and die from infection. On our trek a woman suffered a ruptured spleen after falling out of a wagon. If that had happened 150 years ago, she would have been dead within days. In our case, a helicopter flew in, picked her up, took her to a hospital, and, thanks to modern medical treatment, she was just fine.

One of the stark discoveries for me was that it took so much time to perform the basic tasks of horse-drawn travel—to get ready to move out in the morning, to move along the trail a few miles, and then, when we got into camp, to break the wagon train down, get the horses cleaned up, fed, and watered, build the camp, and fix dinner. By the time 7:30 or 8:00 in the evening rolled around, all I wanted was to find a piece of grass, lie down, and die. There was no energy left to do anything else.

I remember what a sense of accomplishment it was to travel twenty-two miles, the longest distance we had covered in a single day up to that point. And then came the startling realization that in my car on a wide-open western highway I could easily have covered those miles in about eighteen minutes.

I also realized that, in one sense, people did have more time on their hands in pioneer times, but it was a different kind of time. They were forced to sit or ride or work at simple tasks for hours on end. My sore muscles and aching bones testified to that. But during that repetitious activity over long periods of time, the pioneers had more time than we do to think, to let their minds work, to ponder, to dream. So it was a somewhat sad event when we had to leave the wagon train on the last day and return to the world where things were moving so fast. It was time to get back on the treadmill.

Life in the Age of Timelock

As we know all too well, that treadmill is running at a fast pace these days. It's not just our imagination. Today's society is definitely into speed. Because of the pace with which things go now, we tend to do things quickly. For example, if my great-grandfather missed the daily departure of the pioneer wagon train that took him west, he could easily catch up with it on foot. If my grandfather missed his train, it wasn't any big deal; he would wait twenty-four hours and catch the next one. If my father missed an airplane, he wasn't upset; he would wait a few hours and catch the next flight. But if I miss the next section of a revolving door, I go nuts. Why is that? Why are we in such a hurry? Are we afraid we're going to miss something?

Recent national surveys show that in the past few years highway speeds in America have increased dramatically, and not just because Congress allowed states to raise speed limits. The speed limits are often ignored anyway; drivers put the pedal to the metal in what almost seems like a daily stock car race in some communities. I'm no timid soul when it comes to driving, but I marvel at drivers on congested urban freeways traveling at speeds usually seen on the German autobahns; they career through construction zones up to twenty miles per hour above the posted speed limits, dodging in and out of traffic with driving behavior that a decade ago would have landed them in jail.

In many large urban areas, rush hour often approaches gridlock, the condition where traffic is so congested it can no longer move. Ralph Keyes, a researcher and author of *Timelock*, wrote a fascinating book in 1991 in which he describes "timelock," the concept of vehicular gridlock applied to our use of time. "Timelock is the condition that occurs when claims on our time have grown so demanding that we feel it's impossible to wring one more second out of a crowded calendar," Keyes wrote. In the words of one of the respondents to his survey, "You prioritize, list your 'musts,' then you can't even get to your musts."

One of our seminar participants later wrote of his life before learning the What Matters Most process. He described the feelings most of us deal with in the age of timelock:

> I had no control of the events of my life. I labored fruitlessly to meet deadlines. Over-commitment and forgetfulness were traits that were well becoming my hallmark. On a daily basis I would step into the running shoes of good intentions, position myself into the starting blocks of high and often lofty ambitions. Then I would run the race, a race of futility. No matter how hard I tried or redirected my efforts I was always running to catch up with the pack. The finish line was never in sight and

I deeply believed that my stamina would never be enough to help me finish the race.

Sound familiar? Life wasn't supposed to be this way, was it? In the past century weren't all those labor-saving devices invented so that we would have more time for leisure or other things we really want to do?

Our growing use of personal computers provides a case in point. It's hard to believe that little more than two decades ago most people had never even heard of "personal computers." Today, computers have replaced typewriters and other office equipment in most businesses, organizations, and homes. When was the last time you used a typewriter for something other than maybe addressing an envelope? For most of us the personal computer has made it possible to quickly and accurately perform tasks that a few years ago required lab-coated "computer specialists" working in "clean rooms" full of mysterious equipment with blinking lights and low electronic hums.

A good friend in the creative services industry described both the revolution that computers have created in the graphic design and media development fields and also the downside in terms of what happened to the time those computers were supposed to save their users:

Before 1985, preparing a graphic design project for printing was a time-consuming task. First you had to figure out about how much space would be needed on the page for a block of text after it was set in type. Then you had to mark up the text with notations on what size type should be used, the type font you wanted it to be set in, how long the lines should be, how paragraph indents should be handled, and so on. You then sent the marked copy off to have the type set by a typesetting service bureau. When they returned the typeset proofs, you had to check to make sure there were no typos, and you then pasted the type in place with glue or wax. If you were lucky, the block of type fit in the space you had defined. If not, you could hand-edit by cutting and carefully repasting the type, or you could send it back to be redone hours or days later.

Now, my friend notes, all that has changed. The entire task can be done today in just a few minutes on a personal computer, with the results displayed on the monitor exactly as they will appear in print. If the size of the type is too large or too small, it can be changed with the click of a mouse. Do words need to be deleted in order to fit in the space, or are there typos that need to be corrected? No problem. Just select the word or words with the mouse, delete them, or type in the necessary corrections in less time than it takes to talk about it. You can even place electronic versions of photographs on the page and resize or crop them until things look right. And you can instantly print out your pages on a laser printer that does a better job than most large offset printers did a few years ago.

Sounds pretty good, doesn't it? For creative professionals, computers eliminated most of the tedious and time-consuming work and made it possible to do higher-quality graphic design in far less time than was dreamed possible when my friend began his career in the 1960s. But as I mentioned, there's a downside. My friend said,

> The problem lies in the fact that because you *can* do work faster, clients have come to expect you to produce, as a matter of course, what would have been totally impossible in terms of time a few years ago. So even though you've saved yourself all this time compared to the way things used to be, you're just expected to get more work done with that additional time. I feel far more harried today than I did when things took much longer to produce. What's gone is the time to reflect on what I'm doing, to let my subconscious mind work on a design problem and find better solutions.

People I teach say the same thing. Computers, faxes, copiers, networks, optical character readers, and other office innovations were supposed to save us time, which we could then use for other things. "I feel like I'm in a pressure cooker," a harried seminar participant told me. "When you pull a miracle out of the hat one day, it becomes expected performance the next day. There are days when I feel as though I've spent it meeting everybody else's needs except my own."

It used to be that when the pressures got too great, you could escape to a quiet place or leave the office and bask in the silence and privacy of the drive home. Not these days. Our communications technology goes with us everywhere we go. Cell phones ring, pagers beep, and email beckons us on the laptop computer. The drive home used to be a time to escape the phone and collect our brains, but now the car is just an extension of the office as we conduct business, solve problems, check out leads, check with our broker, get the shopping list for the stop at the market, and otherwise continue the rat race.

Not even in our times of leisure do we seem capable of stopping the communications flood. Because the technology allows us to do it, we place cell phone calls from mountain lakes, miles from the nearest town and at times when we are supposed to be getting away from civilization and its demands. Especially with communication technology, it's almost as if, since we have it, we gotta use it. Who can resist the urge to pick up a ringing telephone? It may be something important. I plead guilty along with everyone else.

A good part of the problem has to do with what I have long called "the tyranny of the urgent." The telephone urgently rings in our ears. We can't ignore it, and if we do, we find ourselves distracted with speculation as to who had called and what the person wanted. The intercom buzzes and the message is that you're needed at a quickly called meeting of the company benefits committee. One of your direct reports walks in the door with a problem he could probably solve but has brought to you. A coworker buttonholes you in the hall to bend your ear with the latest office gossip. And to add to the urgency, that make-work report the boss wanted first thing tomorrow morning still hasn't been started, and it's already 4:30.

The problem with most urgencies is that they cannot be ignored. Some of them are important, and a few of them are concerned with things that matter most to us. And yet things that are urgent most often typify the "80/20" rule: They occupy as much as 80 percent of our time, but less than 20 percent usually represent things in our lives that are really important.

Urgencies may also take more subtle forms. Sometimes they form a sort of background noise in our lives. If your life is like most, you have plenty of "have-tos," "shoulds," "ought-tos," and "gottas," many of which probably have little to do with things you attach real importance to.

So how do we compensate for the increasing amount of urgency in our lives? Most of us work harder, beating our heads against the wall trying to get through it. And what happens? If we don't die from stress-related illness or a heart attack, we "lead lives of quiet desperation," in the words of Henry David Thoreau. And we find ourselves saying or thinking, "I just don't ever seem to get anything meaningful done!" or "Is this all there is to life?"

Lessons from the Wagon Train

Our experience with the wagon train concluded when we reached the banks of the Green River in western Wyoming. Those continuing with the wagon train made preparations to move on, while we were driven back to our automobile. Gail and I covered in a few hours the rest of the journey to Salt Lake City, which would take those modern-day pioneers another month or more to complete on foot.

Less than twenty-four hours later I was flying from Salt Lake City to New York. As we flew high above that part of Wyoming over which we had just ridden on horseback, I found myself looking down at the mountains, hills, and sagebrush and remembering my experiences. Now I was flying at nearly 600 miles an hour. In three and one-half hours I would be in New York City, a world away from the wagon train but still feeling all the aches and pains in my body from being in the saddle eight hours a day for ten days. I realized how wonderful it was to live in this day and time. The pace of my life may be greatly accelerated compared to my pioneer ancestors, but my time does not have to be spent toiling just to survive. Knowledge is more readily available, and I can bring technology to bear on the decisions I have to make every day—decisions that will ultimately determine whether I will realize the fulfillment I am searching for in life.

To me the idea of an earlier era when there was more time is a myth. Hectic as the days of our own lives may seem to us, we are given the same daily allotment of twenty-four hours that our ancestors had. The big difference is that we have many more options when it comes to choosing how we will use those twenty-four hours. Freed from the daily struggle just to exist, we can let our time be filled with meaningless activity and motion or spend it doing things that matter most to us.

We do have to make choices: how we're going to spend our time, with whom we are going to spend it, and also what we're going to spend our money on. We must choose what we want to commit to emotionally. It is more important than ever to recognize the power of choice. In the midst of all the confusing choices available during the times in which we live, we still have the power to choose our own destiny, to choose where we are going.

The bottom line is that we can be in control of our lives, and that control comes partly from realizing that we are constantly making choices. When people say, "I don't have time," what they're really saying is "I value something else more." Understanding that fact is a critical element in getting one's life in order. If someone were to ask me to have lunch with him tomorrow and I said to him, "I don't have time," what I'm really saying is "I value some other event more than having lunch with you." It is not polite to say that. It's probably okay to say, "Well, gee, I really don't have time tomorrow," but we should understand that a prioritization has taken place. When your nine-year-old comes up to you as you arrive home from work and says, "Dad, can we play catch?" and your response is "I don't have time," what you are saying is that you value something else more at that particular moment than playing catch with him. If you stop to realize that you've just made reading the newspaper or unwinding for the next thirty minutes more important than playing catch, you may find yourself making a different decision. After dinner if your wife says, "Would you mind helping me with the dishes?" and you say you don't have time, remember that what you're actually saying is "I value something else more than helping you with the dishes."

People often tell me that they have no choice but to have two jobs. And I say, "Why must you have two jobs?"

"Well, I have a big mortgage, I have three kids in college, and I have these cars to pay for."

The fact is, they have chosen that lifestyle. My response is "Well, why don't you sell the big house, buy a smaller house, go down to two cars instead of four, and get your kids to pay for their own college education?"

People are sometimes stunned by that response. It's almost as if they are thinking, "Do you mean I have that option?"

In this and countless other situations, we do have options. And the choices we make, including those about time, are a matter of deciding what really matters to us.

Chapter 3

"Someday I'm Going to . . ."

If one advances in the direction of his dreams, and endeavors to live the life which he has imagined, he will meet with a success unexpected in common hours.

—*Henry David Thoreau*

Have you ever found yourself saying something like this: "Someday I'm going to write a book [or travel around the world or compose a symphony or run the white water rapids of the Grand Canyon or spend a year helping people in South America or any of thousands of things you would someday like to do]?" You're not alone. I imagine that almost all of us have daydreamed about something we would like to do someday. Perhaps it's having more time to be with friends or family, or perhaps it's doing something in an entirely different career. Maybe it's having more time to smell the roses or to pursue an enjoyable hobby or avocation.

However you would finish the statement that makes up the title of this chapter, please be aware that those feelings and dreams of what you would like to do are important clues in identifying what really matters most to you. In this chapter we'll help you write down some of those "someday" things. They will serve to guide you in the deeper digging that we'll do in the chapters that follow.

Since I started my business career over thirty years ago, I have spent an inordinate amount of time on airplanes. It didn't take long before the novelty of air travel wore off, and over time I developed the ability to sleep on an airplane. That ability has helped make the number of hours I spend in the air tolerable, especially when the flights are long.

But when I'm not sleeping on the plane, the time passes faster if I think about something rather than put my mind in neutral. Over the years I have used many of those hours to do some introspection about my life and where I have been and where I am going. In fact, I have developed a wonderful game that has helped make the hours pass more swiftly in airline seats.

My game consists of creating fantasies about things that would be fun to accomplish. Many of those fantasies have been fun to think about but not necessarily attainable, such as what I would do if I were the president of the United States or the premier of China or the prime minister of Israel or (one of my more exciting fantasies) king of the world for just one year. What would I do with the power of being the absolute monarch on the earth? For me, at least, those are fun things to think about.

One sobering and instructive fantasy I have developed is this: What would I do with my life if I were given a second chance on the planet? What if I came back to earth for a second chance? This fantasy is especially sobering to think about if I were not only given a second chance but could also remember the details of my first experience. I have been on the earth now for fifty-five years. What if I died tomorrow, came back at age twenty-one and was told that I had another fifty years to live. What would I do with that fifty years?

The fun part of this mental exercise is conjecturing about what I might do between the ages of twenty-one and fifty-five in my new life. How wonderful it would be to have a young body again—one with no bad knees or ankles or sore shoulders or any of the maladies I am now experiencing! And how great it would be to avoid some of those experiences that were painful or heart wrenching or caused economic difficulties. Then again, the important lessons provided by those experiences would not have been learned, and I would be much less the wiser for that.

But where it starts to get really sobering is thinking about what I would do after age fifty-five, the point where I now sit facing the rest of my life on my first round, the only round I'll really have here.

Clearly I have done some things that I would not want to repeat on a second try and would take steps to ensure that I didn't make those same mistakes again. As George Santayana said about society as a whole, "Those who do not remember the past are condemned to relive it."

I won't bore you with the details of my airborne musings about personal fantasies, but let me reiterate that it is both instructive and valuable to think about having an opportunity to live your life over again.

You may remember *Groundhog Day*, the 1993 film starring Bill Murray as a self-centered TV weatherman named Phil Connors who is given the demeaning assignment of going to Punxsutawney, Pennsylvania, to produce a news feature on Groundhog Day. Punxsutawney is a real place where the citizenry have a special ceremony each year on February 2 to coax the community's resident groundhog, Punxsutawney Phil, from hibernation. The anxious community then waits to see whether or not the groundhog sees his shadow, thereby prophesying the remaining time of winter.

In the movie, weatherman Connors arrives a day early, stays at the local hotel, covers the story the next day, and after doing various things the rest of the day, finally goes to bed at the local hotel. When he wakes up the second morning, he finds himself reliving the previous day. It takes him a little while to realize that he is having exactly the same experiences he had the day before and that he is caught in some kind of time warp. He keeps going to bed each night, wakes up to the same Sonny and Cher song, "I've Got You Babe," on the clock radio, hears the same weather forecast, converses with the same people in the hotel lobby, and interacts with the camera crew and others at the groundhog ceremony. He ultimately ends up reliving this day many times but with the difference I spoke of in my air travel fantasies: with full knowledge of what he had done the day before.

At first he finds this experience fascinating. He tries to see what he can get away with—stealing and doing outrageous acts and stunts. But after a few days he comes to the realization that he might have to relive this same day over again forever, and the soberness of that reality sets in. He steals things and damages property, hoping to get arrested and put in jail to break the pattern. He even tries to commit suicide. Nothing works. He simply awakes once again to the same Sonny and Cher song, the same weather forecast, the same routine of events.

After a while he takes a sober look at his situation and concludes that since he seems to be doomed to live this day over and over for perpetuity, he should at least try to make it a worthwhile day. Through the course of the film he goes from being an arrogant, cocky, ugly personality to a person who learns to care about other people and discovers the power of service in his life. By the end of the movie he has become a totally different human being. That idea—of personal transformation and change in your life—is one I'd like to help you think about here. The trick is to bring about such transformation without having a traumatic experience like the hapless weatherman's in order to trigger it.

When my knees went out on me about five years ago, I took up golf because I could still play it without reinjuring my knees or inflicting other damage on my body. I hope I will be able to play golf until I die. It's a wonderful game, and on a number of occasions I have heard people say that golf is just like life. I wasn't sure what they meant by that until I had played for a couple of years. Then it dawned on me: It is like life because you can totally mess up the fifth hole, but when you go to the tee on the sixth hole, it's like starting over. You have a brand-new experience before you, just like Bill Murray's weatherman character. You are not necessarily doomed to relive the fifth hole (although too often that's exactly what I seem to do).

Similarly, every morning when the alarm goes off we have a totally new opportunity to do what we want with the hours we have been gifted. And we are gifted with that clean slate every day for the rest of our lives. The fact is that we really do get "do-overs" in this life. I may have ten, fifteen, twenty, or thirty years left. What am I going to do with that time? As much fun as it is to fantasize about having a second opportunity on the planet, we both know I'm not going to get that second opportunity, and neither are you. The issue then becomes: *What am I going to do with the rest of my life?* Am I going to continue to kid myself that someday I'll get time to do some of the things that really matter to me? In reality that time will not come unless I decide the time is today.

Sometimes the issue of what to do with the rest of our lives is thrust upon us by events. A participant in one of our seminars a few years ago wrote that he had come to the class after being diagnosed with cancer and "felt that I needed to be sure that my life counted for something before I died."

In several of the workshops I teach we have an exercise that helps seminar participants identify things that really matter to them. Before we break for lunch, we ask them to write on a card something they would really like to do if time and money were no object. At the end of the day we read those cards to the class. It's quite a stirring moment in the workshop when the participants listen to everyone's responses. It's exciting and informative to hear such things as these:

- I would build furniture for my house that would last for generations.
- I would learn Chinese.
- I would save a million dollars.
- I would study history, learn to draw, have fun painting, learn to knit, be an interior designer, be an engineer, be an actor, get married every so often (to the same guy), travel, travel, travel, play more.
- I would eat every meal with friends and family.
- I would bicycle across the country, meeting people and recording their stories.
- I would get enough sleep.
- I would run the New York City Marathon.
- I would take flying lessons to become a pilot.
- I would build my dream house by hand, utilizing only myself and my wife's talents.
- I would volunteer my time working with children in need.
- I would go back to college.
- I would be a character actor on Broadway.
- I would ask all the questions I might normally be afraid to ask, and answer truthfully all the questions asked of me (knowing that people would have the time to understand my answers).

The breadth and variety of the responses is a striking indicator of the wonderful differences in interests, temperament, and personality that exist among all of us. These responses illustrate that at the center of our being there really are things we have a huge desire to do or accomplish. We keep putting those things off because we live in a frenetic, busy world and tend to spend most of our time reacting to the demands of external influences, other people, financial problems, physical ailments, and so on. We never sit down and say, "You know, this is what I would really like to do. When am I going to do it?"

It is my opinion that life's real fulfillment comes when we honestly answer these questions: What really matters most to me? What would I really like to accomplish? What legacy would I like to leave behind? The challenge is to discover what that is and then start doing something about it every day. Whether we're twenty, thirty-five, fifty-five, or even seventy-five, we must consider the time we have left on the planet and when we are going to get started.

What Do You Want to Do Someday?

I'd like to recommend that you take a few minutes now to let your mind play over the "someday" possibilities that interest you. Jot down a note or two describing what you'd do. Don't worry about how far out they may seem or whether they are things you "should" want to do. If they are important to you, that's all the reason you need to include them on your list. The resulting list will be a great help to you as we move into the following chapters because your "someday" dreams will tell you a lot about the things that really matter most to you.

Now that you've identified some of the things you'd like to do someday, think about what you're actually doing concerning any of them. Like many people, you may never get beyond the someday stage; too much of your life is consumed in busyness or undirected activity. Even when we seem to bury our dreams under talk about "being realistic" or protests about "I don't have the time to think about it," there's a part of our inner being that feels a bit of an ache, a wistful feeling that says, "How I wish I could do it."

At this point the deep-rooted questions within each of us may start to surface: Where am I going? Why am I going there? Do I want to go there? Where would I really rather be going? What sacrifice or what price am I willing to pay to get there?

Why New Year Resolutions Don't Work

As each year draws to a close, we as a society go through a little ritual about those "someday" goals. In the week between Christmas and New Year's Day we give thought to how we will be a better person and how we will write differently on the clean slate that will be handed to us on January 1. If we're really serious, we produce a tidy list of things we've resolved to do in the year ahead.

The mental process behind this phenomenon seems to work like this: *This year it will be different. I really will start saving for retirement. I really will lose weight and keep it off. I really will spend more time with my spouse [or children or best friend]. I really will take that Caribbean cruise. I really will get out of debt.*

But what happens? For the first day or week we stick with our resolve. But sooner or later the old habits creep back in. The list is forgotten, and by early spring this year's resolutions will be out of our minds. An important part of the ritual seems to lie in the assumption that no one actually expects to keep any of the resolutions beyond the first few days of the new year.

Have you ever wondered why everyone makes New Year resolutions but very few turn them into permanent behavior change? After all, our lists usually include many things that are really important to us, things we would like to do or see changed in our lives. Some of them really do matter to us, are deeply held *governing values*, if you will. If that's true, why can't we ever seem to do anything about them?

Part of the problem is that we have the cart before the horse. We think that by simply setting out a few vague goals, behavior changes will miraculously happen. Setting goals is important and necessary, but it's not the place to begin. My suggestion is that you delay writing resolutions until you have identified your governing values.

What are governing values? They are those things in your life that matter most to you, those things without which you would find life meaningless or unfulfilling, those things that lie at the heart of who you are and who you hope to become. When you better understand who you are and what is important to you, your New Year resolutions will be more easily identified, and you will have a fighting chance of accomplishing some of them in the weeks and months ahead.

Pain from the Gap

If you feel a twinge or maybe even a little pain when you think about your most recent set of New Year resolutions or "someday" goals, it's probably because you're not doing much about them. Those twinges are related to the deeper inner pain that comes when you realize the direction your life is heading in is not in accordance with what really matters most to you. I know this because people have told me about their frightening experiences and wake-up calls while commuting to yet another day on the frantic professional treadmill.

This was brought home to one of my colleagues a couple of years ago when a woman came to one of her seminars wearing a scarf. It was evident that she was undergoing chemotherapy and the scarf was covering the fact that she had lost her hair. The woman later wrote to my colleague and explained what she had been going through. She had been diagnosed with breast cancer, had undergone a mastectomy, and was halfway through a six-month chemo cycle. She wrote: "Being diagnosed with cancer turned my life upside down. My prognosis is good. . . . They haven't detected cancer anywhere else. . . . I had also chosen, since being diagnosed, to change careers. I had been toying with the idea of being a teacher, but I couldn't bring myself to leave the high salary of a chemical engineer. Being faced with death made me realize 'money ain't everything'— happiness is."

The pain this woman was feeling is the same we all feel anytime we realize that our lives are out of sync or, like the weatherman in Punxsutawney, we are endlessly repeating an essentially meaningless daily grind. On top of that feeling comes the realization that additional income will not make us feel any better.

There are, of course, many other kinds of pain in our lives. Some are physical—hurting one's back or breaking a leg or cutting a hand or getting sunburned, resulting from accidents or bad judgment. These kinds of pain may hurt like the dickens at the time, but in most instances our body heals and the pain eventually goes away.

The worst pain, the most long-lasting pain, is the kind that happens *internally*. This kind of pain seems to come from two sources: unwanted events in our lives, especially those affecting people we love, and the gap between what we really value and what we are doing.

Gail and I went through a very difficult time a number of years ago when we lost a daughter and a granddaughter in a tragic automobile accident. That was a very painful experience, the kind of pain that never totally goes away. There is also the pain of seeing someone, a close friend or loved one, become ill. We also experience inner pain when someone we care about loses a job, goes through a divorce, or suffers some other tragedy that causes them pain. Even though it may not be physically happening to us, we experience the pain. It can be psychological, emotional, or spiritual pain—but it's still real pain.

Perhaps the most excruciating kind of pain comes from the gap—in some instances a wide chasm—between what we really value and what we are doing. This occurs when we realize that we are not living up to our potential or, even worse, that what we are doing doesn't match or is completely in opposition to what we really value, to what matters most to us. The only way to alleviate that pain is to close the gap inside us, just as we must close the gap of a wound in order for it to heal and for the pain to go away.

The primary objective of this book is to *help you close the gap*. Remember that idea. Burn it into your memory. Wake up each morning and ask yourself, "What am I going to do today to close the gap between what I am doing and what really matters most to me?" The next several chapters will help you determine what matters most to you.

Part Two

Discover What Matters Most to You

Descend down into thine own heart and there read what thou
art and what thou shalt be.

Jemima Wilkinson

I N 1785, four years after the end of the American Revolutionary War, representatives of the thirteen newly independent states met in Philadelphia to discuss problems arising out of the Articles of Confederation, the nation's original governing document. Their initial meeting led to additional meetings that lasted for over two years. As that original meeting evolved into a full-fledged constitutional convention, these insightful men looked at each other and, in effect, asked these questions: What are the highest priorities in our lives? What rights as citizens do we value the most? What would we go to war for? What would we lay down our lives for?

The men in those meetings sought to forge a government for the new nation that would be unlike any in existence. Coming out of the painful colonial experience and the frustration of dealing with kings and governmental organizations in which they had no voice, they carefully examined the roles that government should play in a nation of free people. Instead of an all-powerful king or executive, they decided on independent yet interrelated roles for an executive branch, a legislative branch, and a judicial branch. No individuals or groups filling those roles would be able to wrest control of the government because a system of checks and balances among the three branches was formulated.

They also looked carefully at the values that had emerged in the long struggle with England. Many of them had already been stated in the Declaration of Independence, which had been signed and delivered to King George III nine years earlier. Those values included the powerful and overarching idea that "all men are created equal, that they are endowed by their Creator with certain unalienable rights, that among these are life, liberty, and the pursuit of happiness." The Declaration also stated that governments derive "their just powers from the consent of the governed, that whenever any form of government becomes destructive of these ends, it is the right of the people to abolish it, and to institute new government." These values, and others already established in the governing documents of some of the thirteen states, lay at the heart of the Philadelphia discussions and the government that arose from them.

So there would be no question in anyone's mind what those governing values and roles meant to the delegates and the states they represented, they described them in writing. Then, at the conclusion of the process, they summarized them in a powerful mission statement for the new United States of America: "We the people of the United States, in order to form a more perfect Union, establish justice, insure domestic tranquility, provide for the common defense, promote the general welfare, and secure the blessings of liberty to ourselves and our posterity, do ordain and establish this Constitution for the United States of America."

That Constitution, signed in 1787 and ratified by the thirteen states shortly thereafter, has endured for more than two hundred years and still governs the most successful and influential democracy in history. Every law enacted by Congress or in any state in this country is ultimately measured against the Constitution for congruity. It still is a reflection of the basic value system of an entire people and the roles that government should play within that value system. While America grew as a nation, that Constitution was amended and changed. Sometimes the amendments were made to clarify and codify the governing values beyond those stated in the Declaration, such as with the Bill of Rights. Other times they reflected additional roles or changed governmental roles that were needed as the nation grew. Americans revere the Constitution and its amendments as one of the country's most important documents, and many other nations have adopted similar forms of government.

The process described in Part Two of this book has much in common with the process that brought into being the United States Constitution. The process is not a new idea, nor did it start with the Constitutional Convention. It is based on ideas that go far back into history and on true and foundational principles. The process has been used consciously or subconsciously by many of the individuals who left great legacies to mankind.

Both nations and individuals can write their own constitutions, and that's what you'll do as you discover what matters most to you. Your personal constitution doesn't have to have lofty language. Let it reflect your personality, your feelings about things, your way of looking at life and events. Your personal constitution will be an important foundation for the rest of your life. (We'll talk more about foundations later in the book.)

The three elements of the process can be represented in what I like to call a "tri-quation." In algebra, an equation shows the relationship between two equal parts. In similar fashion, we might say that a tri-quation expresses the dynamic interrelationships between three equal elements. The What Matters Most tri-quation looks like this:

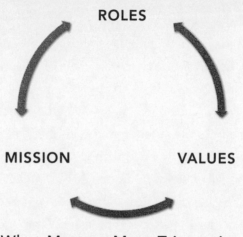

What Matters Most Tri-quation

This tri-quation will help you define what matters most to you, and we'll spend more time on each of the three elements in the chapters that follow.

To start with, each of us will find ourselves filling many roles in life. These may be self-selected roles or ones that are thrust upon us by outside relationships or circumstances. Whatever their origins, these roles impact (and are impacted by) our governing values, those core inner feelings and perceptions that govern much of what we do. Both our roles and our governing values impact (and are impacted by) our personal sense of mission, our feelings about what we should be doing with our lives.

Understanding these three relationships and the powerful way they interact and interrelate will help you identify who you really are and, consequently, what matters most to you.

One of the most powerful aspects of using a tri-quation to show these interrelationships is the way it also represents the importance of balance in our lives. Just as a three-legged stool will not stand with only two legs, the life principles represented by the tri-quation need all three of the elements in order to have structural stability.

The same is true about our lives in general. When I travel, I hear an

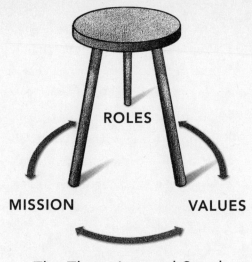

ROLES

MISSION   VALUES

The Three-Legged Stool

increasing cry from people that their lives are out of balance. Many are almost frantic to discover balance in their lives. What I think these people mean by balance is being able to give appropriate time and energy to all the different aspects of life that require (and in many cases *demand*) time and energy from us. For example, take the strong feelings that most of us have with regard to strengthening or building our family relationships. At the same time we may have strong feelings about succeeding financially and personally in a career. Many of us will have feelings about contributing to our community and our nation. Sometimes we have developed altruistic needs. We also need to spend time with our children. These are all reflections of the various roles we play in life and the governing values we hold about them. That's why it can be so painful when we find, for example, that we are spending a great deal of time and effort on our profession but very little time with our family. We are out of balance with regard to one or more of the supporting legs of the tri-quation.

I have long been convinced and have taught that if you really take the time to identify, clarify, and write down your governing values, they will of themselves demand balance in your life. The exciting thing that the tri-quation adds for me is realizing that the roles we play and our inner sense of personal mission also have impact on balance. These three legs—identification of roles, governing values, and personal mission—are all essential for true balance. And the metaphor of the three-legged stool will help you create the desired balance in your life. By identifying roles that matter to you, identifying your governing values (especially as they relate to those roles), and creating your own personal mission statement, you will have a blueprint by which you can achieve balance in your life.

Remember, the stool and the tri-quation are representations of the same principle. You have to have all three legs on the stool in order to sit or stand on it. The same is true of the tri-quation. All three elements are necessary to bring the appropriate balance and control into your life.

Chapter 4

"What E'er Thou Art, Act Well Thy Part"

To thine own self be true, and it must follow, as the night the day, thou canst not then be false to any man.

—*Shakespeare*

An avocation of mine while I was in high school and college was the theater. I thoroughly enjoyed being part of the school productions. While I was in college, I participated in a thirty-minute student television production on the life of Judas Iscariot, the betrayer of Jesus Christ, and I was chosen to play the lead in that production. I can remember vividly trying to get into the role of this person. It was a very depressing experience as I tried to go through the thought processes he might have gone through in making his decision to betray his close friend.

After finishing the production we sat and watched it, and I realized that I had done a very poor job of playing Judas. My first emotion, which is still a vivid one, was one of disappointment at how badly I had done. But the emotion which quickly followed that initial reaction was just the opposite: a feeling of wonder that I had performed the role that badly. The more I thought about it, the more I was grateful that I had not been able to really get into that role, one I would not like to play again.

What Are Roles?

I learned some important lessons from my unhappy experience in the student television production. For one thing, it was difficult to play a role that went against some important inner values I held. I suppose that really good actors can somehow block out their own personal feelings about the person they are portraying, but I couldn't do that. It ended up being a painful experience.

I also realized that there is an important distinction between the roles played in a theatrical production and those played in real life. In the real-life roles you are not making believe; these are the actual roles you possess, however they came to be part of your life. You consciously or unconsciously choose whether you will fill (accept and accomplish) a role. You may fill it partially, depending on its importance to you or your awareness that you have it. Or you may choose not to fill it, either through conscious choice or by default. The important thing to remember is that these life roles are real, not pretend. And because they're real, you must deal with them one way or another.

The kinds of roles we are going to talk about are not the pretend kind; they are real, and we are playing for keeps. The best description I have for these kinds of roles is this: *Our roles are the relationships and responsibilities that we have in life.* Unless we are hermits, we don't live life in a vacuum. There are always other people—family, friends, associates, and others—with whom we interact, often on a daily basis. The relationships and responsibilities we have in those interactions constitute our roles in life.

My brief acting career had an impact on me over the years. Upon reflection I have come to realize that we freely choose to play or not play roles based on our value system. There are some roles that all of us must fill whether we want to or not, such as daughter, son, mother, father, brother, sister, neighbor, member of the human race. We play other roles because of where we are and the particular set of circumstances and experiences life has dealt us; these are such roles as citizen, landowner, refugee, derelict, or sweepstakes winner.

Where Our Roles Come From

A natural human instinct is to want to belong, to have connections to other human beings who share our values or interests. People seek membership in different entities partly because of this need to belong. People join country clubs because they want to belong to something that brings them together with others who have similar social and recreational interests. People join churches and synagogues for religion and also for the sense of community they provide. Having a job is more than a way of earning money; a company or organization also provides a sense of belonging. Kids join gangs because of this intense need to belong and be accepted by their peers. There is security in belonging to something that matters to us, and so we spend a good deal of time and effort seeking or participating as members of many different kinds of clubs, workplaces, organizations, and associations.

You have some memberships whether you want them or not. While you may not have thought of them in this light, you were automatically given membership in four very important organizations the moment you were born:

First of all, you became a member of a dynamic enterprise called Planet Earth. You share that membership with trillions of living creatures as well as all the wonderfully varied and beautiful nonliving things that make up the planet. In this largest membership organization you and all the other living and nonliving things have important roles to play. These roles are related to relationships that, if not honored and filled wisely, could destroy the delicate balance that makes life on earth possible.

Second, you received a membership in the Human Race, more than six billion individuals like yourself, each with his or her own dreams, hopes, aspirations, fears, demons, abilities, and handicaps. Here again we all have roles to fill in order for human society to work. Many of those roles have evolved over thousands of years. Some were founded in our mutual need to respect and cooperate with each other for the general good; others arose naturally out of our individual differences and our varying abilities and desires to contribute to the larger human family.

Your third membership came in being part of a Family. Regardless of your situation, you had a father, a mother, possibly siblings, and other relationships that make up family. We may not relate to roles associated with being part of the earth or even being a member of the human race, but almost all of us have important roles that relate to being someone's son or daughter, brother or sister, aunt or uncle, niece or nephew. Whatever they may be, family relationships and roles change throughout your life. But the necessity of filling one or more of these roles in most cases does not change.

The fourth membership you receive might better be described as a set of membership cards having to do with the Communities to which you belong—your neighborhood, your workplace, your city or town, your region, your state, your nation.

In considering these memberships and the roles that arise out of them, it's important to understand that you bring your own unique life and personality to them. You are truly one of a kind. Your genetic makeup is unique among all who live or have lived on the earth. You are as well quite different in many ways from brothers or sisters with whom you share much of the same genetic code. Even identical twins show physical or personality differences, although almost imperceptible. In addition, your own particular combination of home environment and life experiences have helped shape you beyond the genetic differences, creating the individual living being and personality that is you.

Sensing and understanding your own uniqueness is an important step in the process of discovering who you really are and, consequently, identifying and doing something about what matters most to you. But remember, you extend your uniqueness and individuality beyond yourself only through the roles you fill. As the seventeenth-century poet John Donne said, "No man is an island entire of itself; every man is a piece of the continent, a part of the main. . . . Any man's death diminishes me, because I am involved in Mankind."

Your Roles in Life

Think for a moment about the roles many of us play in the memberships we hold. For example, in our membership as part of the earth, environmentalist is a role that comes readily to mind. Roles such as steward or appreciator of nature or conservationist or explorer or philosopher also have meaning within our membership in Planet Earth.

In our membership in the human race, a number of roles stand out. What would life on earth be like without those who have consciously chosen the role of humanitarian? How much bloodshed has been averted by those who filled the vital role of peacemaker?

As we come to those memberships that fall closer to home, the list rapidly multiplies. In our families almost all of us fill roles called parent, child, sibling, grandparent, and extended family member. Our membership in the communities to which we belong includes roles encompassing almost every field of human endeavor.

You can make your own list of roles that come to mind under each membership category. That list might include some of the ones already mentioned, but there may be others that because of temperament, circumstances, environment, the past, or other factors are almost one-of-a-kind roles. Whatever your roles are, write down as many of them as possible. To help you, here are a few common ones:

Parent	Friend	Son or Daughter
Spouse	Sister or Brother	Grandparent
Partner	Learner	Home Manager
Administrator	Professional	Employee
Nurturer	Observer	Volunteer
Teacher	Peacemaker	Motivator
Listener	Environmentalist	Recorder
Writer	Musician	Artist
Steward	Communicator	Caregiver
Link / Bridge	Colleague	Mentor
Coach	Manager	Provider

In addition to these there is a whole range of "specialty" roles covering the entire spectrum of life and the various activities in which we engage: the kind of work we do, the interests and abilities we have, our particular circumstances and place in the universe. Identify those specialty roles no matter how far out they may seem. The only important thing is that they should be roles with which you identify.

And don't just list the "have-to" roles. Be sure to include roles related to things you'd like to be doing or roles you are not presently involved in but someday want to fill. Your list will be (and should be) unique, a reflection of your life and personality.

Next, take your list of roles and do some consolidating. Maybe minor or "once in a while" roles can be consolidated into one or two "umbrella" ones. Similarly, look for ways to combine related roles into larger chunks, perhaps built around similarities in roles or the place where the role is largely performed (home, work, school, and so forth). It's okay to have many separate roles, but it will be easier to deal with them later if you narrow the list to seven or eight major roles. This is especially true when it comes to planning and functioning in those roles on a daily or weekly basis.

Take an extra hard look at those roles that you may not feel much ownership in and those that are "should do's" being imposed or promoted largely by other people. Keep on your list only those that you feel a legitimate need to fill or be part of. If a role seems to be largely someone else's idea of what you should be doing with your life, be careful about making it one of your "official" roles.

The roles you can clearly choose to fill or not fill are perhaps the easiest to deal with, but in life we must also deal with the roles we didn't particularly choose. Upon closer examination you may find that some roles you think you have to play are not really mandatory. You can make the conscious decision to abandon such a role or modify it to one that fits your own inner values and needs.

Pay special attention to any of the roles that arise strongly out of your own uniqueness, roles that may not be common to others. These are especially important because most likely they lie close to the center of who you really are and are critical keys to understanding who you are and what you would like to do with your life. They may also be the roles through which you will be able to make your greatest contributions.

The Relative Importance of Each Role

At this point I would like to suggest that you look over your list of roles and rank them in their order of importance in your life. This prioritizing can be most helpful when conflicts arise in life, whether in relationships or with regard to events or activities. Having a clearer picture of where each role fits into your larger mix of life roles will suggest the priority that should be given to events and activities. For example, if you feel that your role as a parent has a higher priority than your role as president of the neighborhood book club, there will be less confusion as to what you should do when an important parental responsibility conflicts with the monthly book club meeting.

Throughout your life the roles themselves and the priorities you give them will change. Over time the parental role may diminish in importance relative to other roles, such as that of being nurturer to an ailing parent, a role that may not even have occurred to you in earlier years. Conversely, short-term roles such as the book club presidency may have ended long ago. A major civic role, such as being an elected official, may be a top priority role for a few years but will drop off the screen immediately after that service ceases.

Your roles will also change in priority from day to day. A role related to your career will probably rank high from Monday through Friday, only to be bumped out of its position on the weekend by roles related to being a partner, a parent, or roles related to a hobby, a sport, or other non-work interest. As you rank them now, look at the larger picture and the relative importance of each role in the larger pattern of your life as your life is at this moment. This prioritizing will be helpful later on when we talk about doing something about what matters most to you.

How Well Do You Fill Your Roles?

Once you have identified your major roles, the issue becomes how well you fill them. What kind of performance have you been giving to date? Are you getting rave reviews in some of them? Are there a few that your inner critic would have to give a "thumbs down" to?

Maybe you should rate your performance in each role as you would rate a movie or theatrical production, giving a range of scores from one star to five stars. If you're like me, your critical review will probably be a mixed bag—some successes, some only so-so, a few where you are definitely flopping.

Use your critical reviews to refine your list. Why is performance subpar in some roles? Is it because of lack of time? Lack of ownership or commitment? Again, use a critical eye to see if any of the roles can be eliminated, especially if you are feeling overwhelmed by many roles.

Conversely, look closely at those roles where you give yourself a standing ovation or, if you're more modest, where you feel yourself to be most successful. What is it about those roles that help you perform successfully? What satisfactions do you feel with such a performance? Is the success because of the things you do in the role or the way in which your performance makes you feel? Is it both? These and other questions you ask about your roles will tell you a lot about what makes you tick and will help you identify your governing values, the subject of our next chapter.

Perhaps you've identified some roles you didn't even realize you have. A woman who attended one of our seminars wrote about her self-discovery in this respect:

> What impacted me most about your class was the fact that I realized that *I am my daughter's role model*. What a responsibility! I now show patience towards my daughter, as opposed to rushing her through her meals and not taking the time to stand still and look her in the eye when she wants to talk. I no longer accept phone calls in the evening until after she's gone to bed, and make sure I spend at least one uninterrupted hour with her each evening.

". . . Act Well Thy Part"

Let me return to my theatrical metaphor to recount the experience of David O. McKay, a great spiritual leader and teacher who was a source of inspiration to me in my formative years. In the early years of the twentieth century David McKay found himself in Stirling, Scotland, one of the ancient seats of the Scottish kings. He was far from home, working among people who did not care about the things he was trying to teach them. He was cold, hungry, and discouraged, ready to give up. Walking down an old street of the town, he looked up to see an inscription carved in stone above a doorway: "What e'er thou art, act well thy part."

More than six decades later, after he had become a major spiritual and moral leader and near the end of a long life of service, I heard this man speak of his experience in Scotland. He talked about the abrupt change in perspective that the inscription over the doorway had given him at a critical time in his life. He had never thought that he was filling a role in his life. Something deep inside him responded to the admonition of the inscription, and reading it proved to be a turning point. It inspired him to do his utmost to accomplish his work in Scotland, and it continued to inspire him through a lifetime of service to others.

That experience and the words of the inscription have stayed with me over the years of my own life, and I commend it to you: *What e'er thou art—whatever you hope to be—act well thy part.*

Chapter 5

What Are Your Governing Values?

Without values there is confusion and chaos. When values disintegrate, everything disintegrates. Health disintegrates, poverty attains dominance over affluence, societies and civilizations crumble. When we pay attention to these values that society has always held sacred, then order emerges out of chaos, and the field of pure potentiality inside us becomes all-powerful, creating anything it desires.

—*Deepak Chopra*

Can you honestly say that yesterday's four meetings "at work" were about work you value in life? Think back. Hard. Through each of those meetings, did you sleepwalk? Or did you make a distinct . . . contribution consistent with big things in this life that you value as a unique individual?

—*Tom Peters*

It's time now to turn our attention to the second part of our tri-quation—governing values. As mentioned earlier in this book, our governing values lie at the very center of who we are. Because they are such a core part of our being, they are difficult to define precisely. Some of them might represent various character traits such as honesty, compassion, decisiveness, or generosity that have come to have special meaning or desirability. Others may reflect our attitudes about people or other aspects of our lives, running the gamut from being a loving partner or a caring friend to appreciating nature, having faith in a higher power, or having freedom of action and thought.

Perhaps the best definition of governing values is *what we believe to be of greatest importance and of highest priority in our lives.* They are different for each person. How well you are able to identify your governing values will determine the degree to which you will come to know and understand the real you.

Bubble Gum Cards

At what age do governing values start to have an impact on our lives? You may be surprised at how early in life that is. Let me share an experience with you to illustrate what I'm talking about:

When I was about eight or nine years old, I remember going into a little supermarket in Manoa Valley just outside Honolulu where I grew up. Back in the early 1950s collecting bubble gum athletic picture cards was a big deal. This was years before such cards became "collectibles," and stores and catalogs dealing in them were not even dreamed of. For a nickel at the Toyo Superette in Manoa Valley you could buy a colorfully wrapped packet of cards featuring major league baseball players: a flat piece of bubble gum was included. You'd chew the bubble gum and then trade the pictures to try to get your favorite athletes.

I had a newspaper route but didn't make a lot of money, and I desperately wanted a collection of those cards like most young boys my age had at the time. I went into the little market and proceeded to steal eight or ten of those baseball picture card packets. I tucked them into my pocket and discreetly left the store. (The event is still vivid in my memory.)

I was very excited about getting all those cards for nothing. I brought them home, had dinner, went into my room, took them out, and put them under my pillow so that no one would see them. At first there was excitement at all the wonderful cards I had. Then I began to experience an emotional pain about what I had done, a distinct fear that I would be put in jail if anybody discovered what I had done. I was also afraid that my parents would find out, and I remember feeling a terrible sense of shame and horror. The interesting thing about the pain is that it was a very physical experience, as if there were a hot burning coal in the middle of my chest and I was unable to quench the fire. I agonized over this for several hours there in my bedroom all by myself.

Even at that young age I had a pretty good idea what the source of the pain was and why I was going through all the trauma. I'm sure I didn't understand what emotional trauma was, but I was in real agony and wasn't sure what I should do about it. Finally, about three o'clock in the morning, I made my way down the darkened hall into the bedroom of my parents. Through uncontrollable tears I confessed this grievous thing I had done.

I remember being surprised that my parents didn't react violently and yell at me or spank me for what I had done. Instead, they appeared to be very understanding. My mother got up, sat on the edge of the bed, looked at me, and said, "Well, what are we going to do about it?"

I can still recall the terror of realizing that I would have to take the cards back to the owner of the store, explain that I had stolen them, and hand them back to him. But through my tears I said, "We have to take them back."

My mother replied, "That's fine. I'll drive you to the store. Get some sleep, and we'll take care of it in the morning."

I went back to my bedroom experiencing for the first time in several hours a little relief from the pain. It didn't all go away by any means, because now the fear of having to face the proprietor of Toyo Superette began to flood my system. I don't believe I slept the entire night.

First thing after breakfast the next morning my mother and I drove to Manoa and we walked into the Toyo Superette. I can still see the expression on the manager's face as I presented my ill-gotten bubble gum cards and explained that I had stolen them the afternoon before. I apologized and handed him the cards.

At that point I fully expected that I would spend the rest of my life in jail. But the manager didn't call the police. Instead, he graciously thanked me for returning the cards, thanked my mother, and went about his business. We returned to the car. As I got into the backseat, I had the most wonderful feeling of relief. The pain went away. The burning in my chest went away. The fear of going to jail went away. The agony about what I had done went away. A wonderful feeling of inner peace settled in.

Looking back on that experience, I have a clear view of what happened. Somewhere in my first eight or nine years I had been taught to place a value on integrity and honesty. Young as I was then, those things mattered to me. I'm sure I could never have explained what integrity was all about then, but I knew that stealing was wrong and that somehow it had become important to me to be honest. When I violated that value, when my behavior became inconsistent with that value, it caused me serious and traumatic pain. The discovery of what had caused my pain did not consciously dawn on me until I was older, but honesty and integrity in myself and others have mattered a lot to me ever since. Whenever I have been less than completely honest with other people, some of that pain comes back to remind me about how deeply this value is entrenched in me.

You can probably look back on similar childhood events related to things that still matter deeply to you. There isn't a person breathing who doesn't have a set of governing values that were picked up somewhere over the years. And when our behavior goes contrary to those values, we experience pain.

Why do we experience this pain? Psychologists would probably attribute it to cognitive dissonance, the situation that occurs when our minds try to do the mental juggling and resolve the inner conflicts produced by dealing with two conflicting concepts—in my case the difference between deeply held values and behavior that went completely against those values. Because the pain is caused by the gap between what we value and what we're doing, the only way we can bring peace back into our lives is to bring our performance—what we do—back in line with the governing values. Only then do we have a claim to this thing we call inner peace. Let's say that I value being physically fit but find myself weighing three hundred pounds, little of it muscle. I'm experiencing physical, mental, emotional, and social pain. The only way I can get rid of the pain is to do something about the gap between what I'm doing and what I have placed a value on.

Recently I had the opportunity of speaking to the senior management of my firm, about one hundred of our mid- to upper-level managers. I was talking about this issue and describing the learning experience I was having writing this book. Having contemplated some of the mistakes I have made in my personal and professional life, I made two statements that I felt qualified to share with them, and I asked them to write them down. The first statement was this: "What we do depends on how we feel about what we know."

Now what does that mean? There probably aren't too many smokers in the world who don't know that tobacco isn't good for the human body, but they still smoke (and I realize that the addictive power of nicotine probably has a lot to do with it). I would guess that most smokers know intellectually that smoking endangers their health, but their continuing may have something to do with how they feel about that information. If they feel it is of vital importance to their health, they are more likely to quit smoking. Feeling strongly about it often enables people to overcome the effects of addiction. If, on the other hand, they feel the information isn't important or that it doesn't apply to them, or they have doubts about its truthfulness, they will do little with the information. Even more dangerous is the tendency of some to think that the information may be generally true but that "it doesn't apply to me." *What we do depends on how we feel about what we know.*

Another example: People know that lying is wrong and will ultimately cause serious problems in their lives and the lives of others. Still, many people regularly tell lies, and some of them occupy positions of great trust and responsibility. Several who are persistently untruthful may feel that "it's okay to lie about certain things" or "lying is justified if it gets me what I want." Others may feel that "no one will ever know" or even inwardly ask, "What's the big deal?" *What we do depends on how we feel about what we know.*

The second statement I shared with our managers was this: "When we allow our performance to be incongruent with our governing values, it is excruciatingly painful and palpably stupid." I got a few chuckles when I used those particular terms, but I believe it is a powerful idea. I also believe that all of us have the ability to bring our performance in line with our governing values once we're aware of the pain. When you bring your performance in line with what you value, you experience an inner sense of peace. I experienced that peace first at age eight and then ever since whenever I was willing to bring and keep what I do in line with what I value. Knowing what I now know, the pain serves as an alarm bell that helps me make the necessary course corrections.

I have experienced the pain, but I have also experienced the wonderful relief and peace just as I felt on that morning when leaving the Toyo Superette after returning the baseball cards. The important thing to understand is that this kind of peace doesn't come by chance. It happens because we decide that we want it to happen and because we bring it about by our actions.

What Identifying Your Governing Values Can Do

Several very interesting things will begin to happen in your life when you discover the magic of the governing value process. The first thing you will discover is that you do have governing values. Second, you will see how they drive much of your behavior. Third, you may find that some of your values are driving behavior that is working contrary to bringing you inner peace. And fourth, you will learn that you *can* eliminate or modify values that are harmful or not working for you. When you are consciously aware of your governing values, you really can make changes to your personal value system.

When you get into this process—actually identifying, clarifying, and starting to write descriptions of what these values are—a renewed sense of power will come into your life. You'll know that you are in charge, that you are the master of your ship, and that you have made some very basic decisions that will help you change behavior that may have been causing pain.

One very important fact must be kept foremost in your mind as you get into this process: Identifying, clarifying, and writing down governing values is not a singular event that you do once in your life and then it's forgotten. This is a very dynamic evolutionary process. Governing values have to be revisited constantly, challenged, thought about, internalized, and worked with.

You'll also discover that the priority of your values can change dramatically depending on where you are in life. On one occasion I received a wonderful letter from a woman who had just had a major restructuring or reorganization of the priority of her governing values. This happened after her last child had graduated from high school, and she found herself in a different family dynamic. As she went through the process of reevaluating her governing values, a value that she had kept at a lower priority her entire life jumped to the top of the list. This woman had always dreamed of having her own business career, and now she realized that she could pursue that career without neglecting important duties in her role as a mother. She wrote about how she was enjoying a wonderful and successful business experience now that her children were grown.

Four Natural Laws About Governing Values

As you begin the process of looking inward and examining your governing values, keep in mind that natural laws are associated with governing values. I define *natural laws* as fundamental patterns of nature and life that human experience and testing have shown to be valid. They describe things as they really are, as opposed to how we think they are or how we wish they were. Natural laws exist and operate whether we believe and accept them or not; like the law of gravity, they just are. We can work with natural laws and live our lives safely and successfully, or we can ignore them or try to fight against them and experience pain and frustration.

At least four natural laws have impact on our behavior as it relates to our inner governing values. Understanding these natural laws helps us understand why we have feelings of frustration and unhappiness when we fail to live in accordance with our governing values—the things that matter most to us.

The first natural law could be stated this way: *Whether we consciously realize it or not, we have inner values that strongly influence our outward behavior.*

At the heart of each of us are some bedrock values and concepts that have probably always been there. Psychologists might say these values came from our early childhood experiences. I like to feel that they are part of the individual endowment bestowed on each of us at birth. Whatever their origins, the important thing is to realize that they are deep inside us and influence how we approach the tasks of living.

The second natural law is an extension of the first: *Our natural inclination is for our actions to be consistent with these deeply held governing values.* That's why we feel pain when our actions are not consistent with our values. It is almost as if we have some sort of inner mechanism that checks what we are doing against the contents of our inner treasure box of governing values. Many of our choices will almost always reflect those governing values unconsciously, especially after we become adults. As children we tend to respond to and act on the basis of our inner feelings about ourselves and the world, but as we grow older we acquire an increasing accumulation of "shoulds,""oughts," and "have-tos" that may tend to cover many of the values of our inner selves. We gradually lose our confidence in our inner compass and look to others for values that seem to be successful.

The third natural law is this: *By identifying and clarifying our governing values, we can tap their power to increase our personal effectiveness.* A very real power and focus comes when you identify something deep within your soul that matters to you a great deal. That power and focus will help you cut through the uncertainties and competing priorities of life to move you toward accomplishing goals that are important to you. Helping you unleash that power is what this book is all about.

Lastly, there is this natural law: *When our behavior is in line with our governing values, we experience inner peace.* This is a restatement of the reward mentioned before. Inner peace is one of our major life objectives, something especially needed and dear to us in the hectic times in which we live.

Where Our Governing Values Come From

Our individual governing values have their origins in many sources and experiences. Some almost seem to arise from our genetic makeup, especially those common ones that come from our membership in the human race. For example, most societies value life itself and feel a sanctity about it. Keeping ourselves alive is one of the foundational needs of our existence, and many people place a higher priority on others' lives than they do on their own. That deep and widely held governing value explains why parents die in order to save their children. It also helps explain behavior such as that following the crash of an airliner in the icy Potomac River in Washington, D.C., a number of years ago. One of the passengers clinging to the wreckage kept passing the rescue line to others in the water and then finally succumbed to the cold only seconds before rescuers reached him. The pilot of the rescue helicopter that ferried survivors to shore wept as he related the story to the news media: "He could have gone on the first trip, but he put everyone else ahead of himself. Everyone."

These common human governing values are also reflected in the many moral laws that have developed, even by widely separated cultures—laws built on respect for life, honesty, integrity, and other elements of the moral fabric that binds us all. These shared human values are the basis for the underlying universal ties of love and caring that exist among us regardless of race or culture.

Others grow naturally out of the roles we fill in our lives. In the role of being a friend, values such as mutual respect, trust, and empathy are important in maintaining a lasting relationship. The role of leader or administrator usually includes values such as integrity, wisdom, and vision.

Many of our governing values are formed during childhood, from our initial awareness of and interaction with parents, siblings, and others in our extended families. We later add values from friends and peers. As we get older, some of our values come from what we might call our "invisible committee"—all those in our past and present who touch our lives. Some of these "committee members" are powerful mentors and heroes who help us discover what is inside us while serving as examples of what is possible in our lives. Others, knowingly or unknowingly, may quietly but insistently let us know what we should be doing with our lives. Parents, siblings, teachers, colleagues, and supervisors at work, perhaps even some who may no longer be alive, have their impact on our governing values. It is important to remember that the most important member of that invisible committee is you. While those on your committee can teach you much, in the end your vote counts more than all of them put together.

And some of your governing values will rise up from the deepest recesses of your being. These are the ones for which you won't be able to identify a source; they just are. They are among the most important because they reflect what matters most to you.

Identify Your Own Governing Values

With all that as prologue, take some time to identify your governing values. It may help to write down one- or two-word statements which identify things that are important to you. Don't worry about getting the words or phrasing absolutely perfect. This won't be your final list. Just concentrate on getting them all written down. You can refine the list later.

These things that are important to you can be people, activities, places, feelings—anything that you identify as important. And remember that you're looking for things that are truly *your* governing values, ones that you feel you have true ownership in.

Feeling a bit overwhelmed or unsure about where to start? You're not alone. It's hard to decide on governing values, in part because they are already deep inside and you may not have ready words to describe them. Here are a few questions that can help:

- What things seem most important about each of the life roles I have identified?
- What people, activities, or things have real importance for me?
- What do I like to do when I'm not under pressure to do other things?
- What would I do if I knew I had only six months to live?
- When my life is over, what will I be glad I did? What would I like my obituary to reflect?
- What talents or special abilities do I have? What do I do really well?
- What do I enjoy sharing with others?
- Are there things that I keep feeling inner promptings to pursue?
- What am I doing during the time that I feel the greatest sense of harmony and inner peace?

- What do I consistently think about being or doing someday?
- To what am I willing to dedicate my life?
- Which of the above reflect what I really want, not just what I think I should do or what others may want me to do?

After you've gone through those questions, answer this one (which at first glance doesn't seem to fit with the others):

- What causes me pain?

The answer may suggest values that are important to you but about which you are doing little or nothing. (Remember what was said earlier about the pain we can feel when our actions are not in accordance with a deeply felt value.)

Try to get everything out on the table and written down. Again, don't worry about the order or the spelling. Just get it down.

Use the "Why Drill" to Refine Your List

A useful and informative tool to use in clarifying what matters most to you is one I call the "Why Drill." You may have forgotten that you have one. Most of us used the Why Drill as kids and found it an effective learning tool. In fact, a good deal of our childhood learning probably came from asking "Why?" As kids, when we didn't get an answer that satisfied us, we repeated the question until we did, often driving our parents and teachers nuts in the process.

The biggest problem with our childhood use of the Why Drill had more to do with our own immaturity than our lack of skill. We didn't know when to use it and when not to use it. After Mom or Dad told us a few times to be quiet and stop asking questions, we learned that it was too powerful a tool for everyday use. It was better saved for times of real need. And by the time we reached adulthood and had found the answers to some of our more important questions, most of us simply forgot about the Why Drill and left it to gather dust in some corner of our mind.

The Why Drill, if dusted off, can be a valuable tool for understanding and prioritizing governing values. After you've completed your initial listing of governing values, use the Why Drill to refine your list. The Why Drill can help you understand just how important a particular value is and why it is important to you. You may find a deeper value at work or one that bridges several of the values you've put on your list. Look for the patterns that emerge in this process: Which values are really stating the same thing but in different ways? Is there a larger value that these and other related values reflect?

Be brutally honest with yourself. You may be surprised at some of your answers. And by the way, there are no "correct" or "appropriate" answers here; these answers are for you and no one else.

So for every governing value you've identified, ask yourself "Why?" and make notes about your answers. Write down the first things that come to mind and pay special attention to the feelings that your answers generate. Questions about your values might sound like the following:

- Why do I spend so much time with this person, activity, or thing?
- Why do I feel so strongly about this value?
- Why do I spend money on things related to this value?
- Why am I pouring so much energy into this project, relationship, or activity?
- Why do I spend so little time or energy on this value? Is it not as important to me as the things on which I do spend my time or energy, or is it important but currently overshadowed by other commitments or urgencies?

This introspective experience can be extremely valuable. In the process of going through the Why Drill you may find that some things aren't as important to you as you had thought. Conversely, something previously thought to be a less important value may surface as something you really do care about.

Keep asking "Why?" until you're satisfied that you've reached the real reason or motivation behind each value. Understanding why you value something will help you see whether it is really important to you or whether you've consciously or unconsciously chosen someone else's value. You may find that several of your values are actually part of a single value that can be expressed at a deeper or more comprehensive level. And the whole exercise will help you when it comes to prioritizing your values. (More about that later.)

Getting to Bedrock

Some values may be important, but you can't clearly identify the reasons. Maybe your response to "Why?" is "Just because." That's okay. Such values are often the most deeply held and rest on your inner bedrock. They are important simply because they are important, and there is no need to further explain or rationalize it.

My colleague and friend Jerry Pulsipher grew up in a small town in the wild red-rock-canyon country of the Southwest until his family moved to an urban community when he was eight. He has lived away from the canyon country ever since, but Jerry still has an extremely strong attachment to the landforms and natural landscape of that starkly beautiful region. He always enjoys spending time there, and he has read widely about its natural and cultural history. There's something about the red-rock country that is "home" to Jerry, something that produces deeply felt emotions. He can't give any better reason for his attachment than "just because."

Once he recognized that this attachment was there at the bedrock level of his being, he let his love of that region work for him rather than against him. He came to realize that it is okay to let that value be there and to let it guide and influence his life's direction. He has also been able to see how that deeply held value can work with many of his other governing values and has consciously changed his vocational goals.

Several years ago Jerry resigned an executive position with our company. Friends and associates asked him how he could walk away from a job that provided good income and security. Since then he has used his writing and artistic talents to plan and develop exhibits for park visitor centers and other facilities to help others learn about and appreciate the cultural and natural history of his beloved red-rock canyons and plateaus. He has also been working on a book that will combine his artistic interpretations of the region with prose that arises out of his deep feelings for this country. He is experiencing creative satisfaction that would not have been possible in his former job with its more formal work surroundings. In a few years he hopes to retire to some corner of his special landscape and spend his remaining years interpreting it for others through art and writing.

As you look at your own governing values, try to arrive at a compact list of things about which you can say, "Yes! These are things I really care about, and I am willing to spend my time, money, and energy on them." Then you have identified your core governing values.

Write a Clarifying Statement

Once you have your compact list of governing values, write each one on a note card or piece of paper and take a moment to write a few sentences that clarify what that value means to you. This may be a more in-depth description of the value, or it may be more of a statement about why it is important to you, or it may be a little of both. Just write it in a meaningful way that will motivate you.

These clarifying statements and the additional details may suggest long-range goals that will lead to the fuller implementation of the value in your life. Also, the next time you review your list, you don't want to find yourself saying, "What did I really mean by that?"

I have found it helpful to state my governing values as affirmations—statements describing how I am when I have that value fully implemented in my life. For example, one of my governing values is "I foster intellectual growth." That doesn't mean I am the world's greatest teacher or that my own intellect has achieved the level of Einstein, but it does summarize a value that is deeply important to me. My clarifying statement for this value reads: *A man can think no deeper than his vocabulary will allow him to. I read regularly each day. I select my reading from the best books and articles of the day. One cannot teach from an empty well.*

Over the years that I've been teaching this process, many others have shared with me their governing values. They are inspiring not only because they state very well what matters most to their authors but also because of the breadth of human interest and endeavor that they encompass.

One man approaching retirement gave special emphasis to one of his important governing values, "Personal responsibility." His clarifying statement for this read:

> I am responsible for what I am, what I do, what I think and how I react. I create my own state. Happiness comes from victory, not from pleasure—victory over self, negativism, self-pity, petty-mindedness, sin and apathy. I listen. I take notes. I absorb ideas. I model great people. I keep my word. I'm truthful. I make commitments sparingly but I keep the ones I make. I constantly build my vocabulary so I can communicate better and improve my IQ and think more deeply. Speech and the ability to express through spoken words, sentences and paragraphs is a precious gift from God; therefore I do not use profanity.

Talk about a blueprint for a successful and fulfilling life!

Another example of an extremely thoughtful governing value came from a woman who recently shared her list with me. The briefly stated value is "I grow intellectually." Her clarifying statement read:

> I listen with an open mind to what people have to say and take in what I think might enhance my world. I read things related to all aspects of my life (job, kids, the world in general) and seek to internalize worthwhile things. I seek opportunities for formal education that will help me learn and grow. I learn everything I can about my department and company that will enhance my ability to do a better job.

That's a rather comprehensive clarification of that value, but I'm sure you can see the depth and power that the value assumes when the additional clarification is written out this way. I can see half a dozen long-range goals in that statement, ready to be extracted and written out to help this person do something about this value in her life.

Another person attending one of my seminars wrote about how the process had helped him discover a governing value that was very important to him—to "lead a disciplined life." His clarifying statement was written as affirmations:

> My life is one of discipline and direction. I control events and order their placement in my daily activities. I am free from the stress caused by a lack of control. Rather, I am free to direct my own course in life and enjoy the benefits of that freedom. I recognize that structure is not a rigid way of life. Structure is simply a firm foundation on which a life of freedom is built. If my foundation is not firm; if the structure is weak; if I am undisciplined, my life is a tottering mess. I live a productive and meaningful life of direction and discipline.

Take some time to write clarifying statements for each of the values that have made it to your final list. Remember, the exact form is not important. You can state your values as affirmations or descriptions, or you can put them any other way. Instead of writing paragraphs like the ones given above, you may be more comfortable writing a simple list, such as this one sent by a recent seminar participant:

> Health [governing value]
> - I work out three times a week for one hour.
> - I limit fast food to no more than once a week.
> - I improve the quality of time spent on weekends.
> - I laugh or smile more often.
> - I identify and mitigate stress sources.

Or perhaps an outline format like this one may better suit your style and temperament:

> I. I will strive to be honest with myself about myself.
>   a. I work at knowing my strengths and limitations in all settings.
>   b. I refuse to lie to myself about my motives for any action or thought
>   c. I strive to know and acknowledge my motives and impulses, no matter how base or noble.

I also like this thoughtful, succinct, and organized expression of a deeply held governing value by the same seminar participant as the previous one:

IX. This life has given me much. It is important to me to return to the world some of what has been given to me.

    a. It is important to me to commit time and resources to serve others in ways comfortable to me.

    b. My community should receive the benefit of my competencies.

    c. Some fraction of my time will be committed to community service.

However you identify and clarify your governing values, the important thing is that they make sense to you, that you know what they mean to you personally.

Prioritize Your Values

Once you have identified what your governing values are, a very important next step is to place them in order of their importance to you. This can be a very difficult task. As you launch into this effort, consider this experience and your possible responses.

Let's suppose that out in front of your house or office, lying on the street, is an I beam, one of those large steel beams used in constructing buildings and highway overpasses. I beams have a cross-section like the typeset letter I, some of them almost like a wide H that is turned on end. The beam's shape gives it great strength. Let's say that this particular I beam is 120 feet long, 6 inches wide on the top and bottom, and about 1 foot high. I'd like you to stand at one end of the I beam, and I'm going to get at the other end. When we're both in position, I pull from my wallet a $100 bill. I shout down to you at the other end of this 120-foot I beam and say, "If you'll walk across this I beam without stepping off either side and get here in less than two minutes, I'll give you this $100." Will you come? My guess is that you'd quickly look at the situation, decide that this is definitely doable, and you'd come across the I beam—an easy $100.

Now let's change the scenario and take this same I beam, put it on

the back of a long flat-bed truck, and drive it all the way to New York City. At the lower end of Manhattan Island there are two famous skyscrapers called the World Trade Center, the tallest twin towers in the world, 1,360 feet high. Continuing our experience in the theater of the mind, let's say that we've mounted on one of these towers a crane that will drop a cable down, pick up the I beam from our truck, lift it up to the top of these two buildings, turn it sideways, and place it in brackets attached firmly to each of these two buildings. These two buildings now sway in unison. (They do sway, by the way. They were designed to sway as much as 30 feet at the top.) So our I beam is now firmly bolted in place between the two buildings, and I invite you to take the elevator to the top of one of the buildings while I take the elevator to the top of the other tower.

Have you ever been to the top of the World Trade Center? It's a magnificent view. Whenever I have been to the top, there has always been a wind blowing. Let's say that there happens to be a wind today of about 40 miles per hour, and to make it even more interesting, it's raining. You're on top of one of the buildings; I'm on the other, 120 feet away. I shout through the wind and the mist and say, "I have a $100 bill. If you'll come across this I beam without stepping off either side, and get here in less than two minutes, I'll give it to you. Will you come?"

I have used this example and asked this question in literally hundreds of seminars, and I have yet to find anyone that would come. I then say, "All right. Instead of $100, I now have $10,000. Would you get on that I beam for $10,000?" Probably not. I now up the ante. I now have $50,000 on my side of the I beam. All you have to do is walk the same 120 feet you walked on out in front of your house on the street. Would you get on the I beam for $50,000? Probably not. I now raise the ante one more time, to $1,000,000. Of course the rain is up and the wind has increased. There are no safety devices, it's a 6-foot-wide I beam, 1,360 feet to the street, a 120-foot walk. Would you come across for $1,000,000? Unless you just happen to be a trained high-wire circus performer, your answer would probably still be no.

Let's change the scenario one last time. Instead of my standing at the other end of the I beam waving that million dollars, your little two-year-old child or grandchild is there. And let's say that no one else is there to help and that the child has climbed up on top of the I beam. She looks across and, delighted to see you on the other side, starts to walk across. At that point I don't need to ask if you will come across the I beam. You would probably run across that I beam or at least find some way to get across it to save your child.

Let's take another look at this sequence of events and see what made the difference in the responses. When the I beam was on the ground, nothing seemed very dangerous. At worst you might have to step off if you lost your balance, and walking that 120 feet seemed like a surprisingly easy way to earn a hundred bucks. But when we moved the I beam to the top of the World Trade Center, even the offer of a million dollars was not enough to outweigh the very real danger added to the equation by the wind, the rain, and that 1,360-foot drop to the street below.

Then why did your motivation change when your child was at the other end of the I beam? The physical danger to you was just as real as it had been when the $1,000,000 had been offered, but you'd go across anyway. The I beam story gives us a dramatic demonstration of the fact that you have already placed some priorities on some of your governing values. The governing value of having sufficient financial means in your life was obviously not as highly valued as the governing value related to the sanctity and preservation of your life, as you learned when confronted with the wind and rain and the

more than a thousand-foot drop. But as strong as the value of self-preservation was, the value of the life of your child or grandchild turned out to be even greater.

What point am I trying to make in all this? As you get into the process of prioritizing your governing values, ask yourself this question: "What would I cross the I beam for?" It's a marvelous question because the governing values you identify are probably those that are most important to you, that matter most to you. And you may find that only two or three of the values on your list will qualify. Of the sixteen governing values I have identified for myself, only four would cause me to attempt that perilous crossing.

After teaching this concept, people have told me all kinds of things that they suddenly realized were of vital importance in their lives. Very often these have to do with families or others with whom strong bonds and relationships are shared. In addition, the I beam experience also helps you learn important things about yourself, some of which you may not have ever before realized. One mother who had been carrying around a lot of excess emotional baggage and had been struggling with feelings of inadequacy said in a moving letter:

> What would I cross the I beam for? Well, I have actually crossed that I beam for my children. Because of this, I realized I did have courage. I could cross that I beam again.

I went home that night and I couldn't get this concept out of my mind. I visualized myself standing at both ends. At one end I saw myself afraid to look at myself. At the other end I saw myself with my arms out and tears flowing down my cheeks reaching for help. With that in mind, I was able to put together my values.

So put yourself on top of the World Trade Center. Look across at the other tower through the wind and rain, test your footing on that narrow I beam, and ask yourself, "What would I cross the I beam for?"

As you can see, it is important to place the values you have identified in their order of priority. If you don't prioritize your values, you may wind up with perplexing decisions to resolve.

Let me illustrate. Two governing values on my list are "I am financially independent" and "I am honest in all things." Now let's assume I'm struggling financially and that someone approaches me with an opportunity that is "100 percent certain" to guarantee my family the long-term financial security they lack. There is one little hitch, though. You guessed it—this opportunity isn't exactly legal, and even though I probably won't get caught, it's not at all ethical.

What do I do? Well, it depends on which value is more important to me. My value of "I am financially independent" is ranked number 12 on my list of values. "I am honest in all things" is number 8. What this reflects is that I want to be financially independent—but only if I don't have to buy that financial independence with dishonesty. Being honest is more important to me than being financially secure.

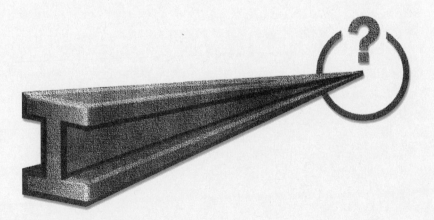

Because I had thought through the relative importance of each of those values and had ranked them accordingly, I would have little difficulty telling the person making a less-than-ethical investment pitch that I wasn't interested.

The best thing about ranking your values is that you do it in advance. You may find yourself having to decide on the spot between two courses of action that may or may not bring you inner peace. When you are not certain what your priorities are, it's easy to rationalize: "Well, my family is important to me. With this money I could give them the security they deserve." Uncertain priorities lead to situations in which actions are not determined by values or principles but by the desirable ends they may produce. We usually call this "the end justifying the means." It happens all the time, and the only cure for it is to clarify in your own mind the priority or ranking of your governing values. Don't wait until an emergency or traumatic event forces the prioritization of your values.

A father who had attended one of our seminars wrote to us about a tragic experience. Writing of his ten-year-old son, he said, "Initially I was a very devoted father, and I stayed very active in his sports by either coaching or assisting in coaching his soccer, basketball, or baseball teams. As my career became more demanding, I lost sight of that and became less of a participant in his life."

This father went on to tell of his son being seriously injured in a car accident and suffering severe brain injuries. According to the surgeons who operated on him, he should have died, but the boy miraculously survived with no complications at all. The father concluded his letter by saying, "It is unfortunate that it sometimes takes things like these to correct the priorities in your life. I can tell you now that my son is my number one value in my life, and I will hopefully never lose sight of that again."

Look at your final list of governing values and their clarifying statements. Then rank or reorder the list to reflect their relative importance to you. Put the most important values at the top of the list, the least important at the bottom. This exercise may require some more soul searching, but I assure you that you will appreciate the benefits of deciding these things now rather than struggling in the heat of the moment.

Can Our Governing Values Be Changed?

If you've been completely honest with yourself in going through this process, you may have found some values that you don't really wish to have. Are you stuck with the basket of values you've identified, or is there a chance that you can trade some of them in for other, more positive values that you've identified?

As you've worked through this process, you may have discovered a few values that didn't get written down—ones that your actions and present directions indicate are there but that you may not want to admit. The positive values, the kind "good people have," always make it to the list, but almost all of us find that some are not so positive or are not ones we wish to have. Some may actually be holding us back from realizing the full potential of the better side of our personalities.

The values-identifying process can be especially helpful when it comes to values you may have reluctantly admitted you have and would like to change. Being completely honest with yourself and putting a less desirable value on your list will bring it into full view. Then you can deal with it directly. You can take a closer look and try to understand why such a value is there, and you can make decisions and set some goals to do something about it. (We'll talk more about the goal-setting part of the process in the chapter on planning.)

But what about those "good" values about which you are doing little if anything? In talking with people about these values, I find that they often have to do with conflicts between career and family. In surveys conducted over the years about what business executives, men and women, valued most, a high percentage of those interviewed said they valued their families most. And then when asked how they spent their time, it turned out that very little time was actually spent being with or doing things with their families. This would indicate that perhaps they value more than the family, such things as financial success, recognition by professional peers, or almost anything other than family. "My family" was the "right" answer to give for the survey, but it was not what was most important to them.

Many conflicts with family and career values actually relate less to whether you have a "good" or a "not so good" value but the relative importance you have placed on those values. How much value I place on "being successful" will determine how much time and energy I spend in trying to achieve it. If I place a higher priority on values related to career success than those related to family relationships, the career will win out nearly every time.

The wonderful thing about this process is recognizing that you have control over these kinds of issues, over what your governing values are. You can decide that you don't like a particular value. You can decide to add or eliminate a governing value. You can decide to change your interpretation, your understanding, and your definition of a particular value. You can decide that a particular governing value has greater priority in your life than it previously had. That's what separates human beings from the rest of the animal kingdom. We can change our values. Not only that, identifying and clarifying your governing values can be a tremendously liberating experience. It can expand your horizons and help you to see new possibilities in life. When you discover what really matters most, you don't need to pretend or compare yourself with anyone else. You can start being yourself in the truest sense of the phrase. As one seminar participant put it, a woman who was working toward a law degree but was inwardly hating the prospect, "I don't have to pretend to be a lawyer or pretend to want to be a lawyer anymore. I can just be myself. It's so exciting!"

Chapter 6

What Is Your Personal
Mission in Life?

To attempt to climb—to achieve—without a firm objective
in life is to attain nothing.

—Mary Robeling

The most pathetic person in the world is someone who has
sight but has no vision.

—Helen Keller

He who has a why to live for can bear almost any how.

—Nietzsche

MISSION

Years ago I came upon an important statement in the
Old Testament's book of Proverbs: "Where there is
no vision, the people perish." It took me a long time
to understand what that statement really meant.
Speaking of vision in a literal way, imagine yourself driving at
night in the middle of winter. Let's say you are going along the highway doing 65 or 70 miles per hour, and in an instant you find yourself in a dense, thick fog. How do you feel the minute you realize you
can't see more than, say, thirty feet in front of your car? Your initial
response is probably a bit of panic. Most likely, your foot goes immediately to the brake, and you slow the automobile down to a crawl.
You move as slowly as you dare so that you won't run into someone
up ahead and inflict bodily harm on that person, yourself, or your automobile.

Let's take the experience to a more uncomfortable level. Suppose that as you go through the fog it gradually grows thicker and thicker until you can see only two or three of the dashed white lines in front of you. At this point maybe you even find yourself rolling down the window to try to see the lines near your wheels. Few experiences are more panic-producing. You find yourself afraid to stop for fear that someone will plow into you from behind, but you can barely move forward because you really aren't sure if you're going to stay on the road. I've even been in situations where the fog was so thick and disorienting that I didn't know which direction was which. That may be similar to the experiences of aircraft pilots who find themselves inside a cloud and don't know whether they are upside down or right side up.

Next, think about how it feels as you emerge from the fog. At first, instead of just two or three of those white lines in front of you, you can see four, six, or eight of them. Then you can see the next turn in the road, and suddenly the fog totally lifts and your headlights illuminate the road two hundred yards in front of you.

What is your immediate emotional response? In addition to a great sigh of relief and an easing of tensed muscles, most likely your foot immediately goes from the brake to the accelerator. You start to move faster. You stop sweating, dry your hands, put your elbow back on the armrest, turn the radio back on, and find yourself experiencing peace again.

Once you are safely out of the fog, think about the only thing that changed during that experience, an event that may have lasted only a few seconds. The only thing that changed was your vision, your ability to see. With vision you saw the road ahead clearly and felt no distress. When there was no vision, you were, as stated in Proverbs, in danger of perishing.

Are You Living Your Life in a Fog?

All those negative emotions that you experienced while driving in the fog are similar to the emotions you experience when you manage your life the same way. When you have no vision for your life, for your career, for your family, for you personally, for what you want to accomplish—when you have no vision of where you are headed, your emotions are the same as experienced on the foggy highway. Being in a fog about your life is in many ways even worse than the fog on the highway. When driving in the fog, you have a reasonable assurance that it won't go on forever. But there's no assurance that it doesn't go on forever in a life fog.

The lack of personal vision can be physically and emotionally debilitating. You have a hard time getting out of bed. You move sluggishly. You're not excited. There is no anticipation about the day, no looking forward to getting up in the morning. At best, all you want to do is exist and get by. There isn't any fun in life, no sense of fulfillment.

But the minute you create vision in your life—and that's what we're talking about when we talk about discovering what matters most—the energy comes back. You can't wait to get up in the morning. You know exactly where you're going and why you're doing what you're doing. The excitement that comes with that is the same excitement you experienced when you pulled out of the fog, saw the highway, and were willing to step on the gas to get to your destination. With vision there is a sense of urgency, a divine impatience for life. Many great and successful people have expressed this. Remember Winston Churchill at 3 A.M. in England's darkest hour; he was "impatient for the morning."

It is my hope that the exercises we've done so far to help you identify your major roles in life and your most important governing values have produced some of your own "coming out of the fog" feelings about your life.

The Power of Knowing Your Personal Mission in Life

Let's take a deeper look at our metaphor of car headlights and the fog-bound road. When I was a young man I lived for a time in England, a land known for its foggy climate. During that time I found myself more than once driving through thick fog, and I noticed that many British automobiles were equipped with fog lamps—low-slung lights with powerful yellow beams that could cut through the fog to provide a better view of the road than was possible from the headlights alone. I'm not an expert in the science of illumination, but I imagine that the effectiveness of the fog lamps had something to do with both their low placement and their color. Whatever the reason, they markedly improved a driver's ability to see the road ahead on a foggy English night.

In many ways the automobile fog lamp is much like a vision-enhancing tool you can employ in your own life—your *Personal Mission Statement, which is a brief written expression of your overall purpose in life.* That may sound a bit lofty, but when applied to individuals, it is a tool all of us can use, not just famous inventors, gifted writers, or well-known humanitarians. If you think about the idea of a Personal Mission Statement in light of what you have already learned about the roles you have identified in your life and the governing values you have defined for those roles, you'll start to see the connection. Your personal mission in life is all your roles and values distilled into a sentence or two that describe *what you want to be and accomplish in your life.*

Finding the words to describe your unique life purpose will not be easy, but it will definitely be worth it. Once you have determined your personal mission in life, it will become your fog lamp, clearly illuminating the road in front of you and helping you cut through the fog of everyday concerns and activities.

The importance of having a Personal Mission Statement dawned on me only within the last several years as I became acquainted with the concepts taught by my colleague and friend Stephen Covey. After learning more about the idea of having a Personal Mission Statement, I realized that I had had one for a long time; I just hadn't thought of it in those specific terms.

My Personal Mission Statement was put into words for me by one of my personal heroes, Winston Churchill. When I was living in England, I had an opportunity to hear Churchill speak. It was near the end of his life, and he spoke of the history he had witnessed and in which he had played such a powerful part. But what jumped out at me in that address was a statement he made about being motivated by the desire to make a difference, to leave the world a better place.

That idea—to make a difference—struck a powerful chord deep within me, and I made a commitment to do that to the best of my ability. That commitment has guided much of what I have done, the causes I have espoused, and the contributions I have tried to make in my professional and personal endeavors. In my Personal Mission Statement are Churchill's words—*"make a difference."*

Writing Your Personal Mission Statement

If you have completed the exercises previously outlined, you have identified the many roles you play in your life and some of the governing values you hold about those roles. The third step in the process is to synthesize what you have written into a concise statement of your personal mission in life.

These three elements, all of which work dynamically together, will constitute a preamble to your personal constitution, which is about who you really are. Knowing who you are will enable you to tap the power that flows from that knowledge. You will then be able to determine major life goals and your mission. After that you will select the intermediate steps needed to accomplish those goals and the actions needed to see their fulfillment.

But that's getting ahead of ourselves. The immediate task is to write your mission in life. This can be a two- to three-word statement like mine. It can be written as a song or poetry. Some people have mission statements that go a full page. It doesn't matter how long or short the description of your mission is as long as it defines what that mission is.

To help you in this effort, consider what an empowering mission statement is and does. A Personal Mission Statement . . .

. . . represents the deepest and best within you. It comes out of a solid connection with your inner life.

. . . is the fulfillment of your own unique gifts. It's the expression of your unique capacity to contribute.

. . . is transcendent. It's based on principles of contribution and purpose higher than self.

. . . addresses and integrates all . . . fundamental human needs and capacities. It includes fulfillment in physical, social, mental, and spiritual dimensions.

. . . is based on principles that produce quality-of-life results. Both the ends and means are based on true principles.

. . . deals with both vision and principle-based values. It's not enough to have values without vision; you want to be good, but you want to be good for something. On the other hand, vision without values can create Hitler. An empowering mission statement deals with both character and competence.

. . . deals with all the significant roles in your life. It represents a lifetime balance of persona, family, work, community—whatever roles you feel are yours to fill.

. . . . is written to inspire you, not to impress anyone else. It communicates to you and inspires you on the most essential level.

As Stephen Covey has stated, "We don't invent our missions, we detect them." You can start your own detection process by reviewing the roles and governing values you have already identified. Take a closer look at the roles in which you feel a special connection, that you enjoy, and that you strongly desire to perform well. Look especially at the governing values that seem to relate to many or all your roles. Almost certainly they will have a close relationship to your personal mission in life. It may be helpful to group together roles and governing values that seem to have something in common. You may find it useful to review again the questions on pages 91 to 93 that you asked yourself during the process of identifying your governing values. This time add the following two questions:

- What single thing do I want to be remembered for?
- What is the most important legacy I can leave to family, friends, and associates?

As you do all this, look for the unifying theme, the single thread that helps tie your roles and governing values together. It may take a little digging and a lot of pondering to find this single idea or principle that brings it all together.

There are no right or wrong mission statements, just *your* mission statement. There is no right or wrong way to express your mission. You may wish to state it as an imperative, such as "Succeed at home first," "Serve God and others," or "Leave this world a better place than I found it." Or, if you find that affirmations help you internalize important self-concepts, you may want to state your personal mission in terms like these: "I will use my time, talents, and material possessions to make life more enjoyable and fulfilling for others."

Let me share some examples of what has been included in the mission statements of people I know:

- To create joy
- To have peace
- To make a difference
- To raise a fine family
- To contribute to society
- To bring beauty into people's lives
- To excel in my field
- To find success and fulfillment through purposeful living

As you can see, these examples cover a rather wide range of interests and inner desires. One of the most profound and beautifully worded Personal Mission Statements I have heard is by author Laurie Beth Jones: "To recognize, promote, and inspire the divine connection in myself and others."

Remember, the important thing is to *identify a mission statement that is uniquely yours*. Don't just pick a mission statement from among those I've listed or others you may be aware of, especially if you are doing so largely because of "I should" or "I ought to" feelings. This written summation of what you are and what you want to do should be something you have some passion about, something to which you are willing to dedicate your life. Only then will it become an inner power that will move you toward fulfillment of your inner and unique destiny.

A Mission Statement Can Make a Major Difference in Your Life

Stephen Covey recently shared with me letters he had received from a number of people attending his 7 Habits seminars, in which the concept of Personal Mission Statements are also taught. They mention how identifying and writing a Personal Mission Statement had helped them save relationships that were important in their lives. Excerpts from two of these letters are given below because they illustrate beautifully the life-changing power that can come from shaping what matters most to you into a personal vision of what you want to do and be.

One letter was written by a woman who admitted to having always struggled with taking personal responsibility, finding it "far easier and self-reassuring to blame somebody or something for the way things are—somebody and something other than myself, that is." After writing her Personal Mission Statement, she put it aside and forgot about it. Six months later she read a newspaper article that jogged her memory about the worth of defining a personal mission, and she decided to look at the statement she had written for herself. In her words:

> I picked up my mission statement and read through it. Right in the middle there's this sentence about cherishing the good in my husband. A little voice inside of me challenged: "Well, do you? Do you?" I shrugged it off but made a commitment to read this mission statement every Monday to remind myself of what I was about. So I heard the voice every Monday morning. Every Monday morning, whether I scanned over my mission statement on an airplane or just visually thought about it, these few lines hit me in the face. I heard, "Well, do you? Do you?" and I thought, "Am I actually living by this?" I began to examine myself.

My husband and I are very different people. I'm very struc-
tured, organized and even-tempered. He is just the opposite.
He is unorganized and very headstrong. I suppose some people
would call him intuitive and emotionally liberated. In my attempt to make myself feel good and cast the blame, I had always thought about his qualities in the negative. That way I
could blame him for our problems we encountered together. I
had also come to believe that there was nothing we could do
to resolve these issues; Larry was the way he was. I couldn't
change him.

As I thought about this man I had been married to for
twenty-three years, I started to see him in a different light. I realized that were it not for his freespirited sense of adventure, all
our vacations would have been organized down to the last
minute and rest stop. We would never have discovered the pen-
guins on a little beach in Cape Town or the restaurant overlooking the canal in Amsterdam. When I planned the vacation,
we would know exactly where we were going, where we would
stay, how we were going to get there, and what time we expected to arrive. I also saw that what I had always viewed as his
negative traits were only negative because they were different
from how I would do things. I had always been reluctant to em-
brace things that were different, even if that person were my
husband. In some ways, I had kept him at arm's length for
twenty years.

I returned from that particular trip [when these realizations
came] with a new appreciation for Larry. I could see him in a
completely different light.

Another woman, a divorced mother of four, wrote with a similarly life-changing and empowering experience:

Twenty years ago my husband moved out, and I was left with
four children—ages four, six, eight, and ten. For a while I absolutely lost it. I was devastated. For several days I just lay in bed
and cried. The pain was so deep. And I was so frightened of
what lay ahead for us. I didn't know how I was going to do it.

There were times I would just go from one hour to the next and think, "Well, I didn't cry in this hour. Let's see if I can not cry the next hour." And this was very hard on the children because their dad had just moved out of the house and for a while they thought their mom was "gone" too.

It was the children that finally gave me the strength to pull through. I realized that if I didn't get my act together, not only was I going down the tubes, but I was taking four precious people with me. . . .

I began to realize that I needed a new vision. We were no longer a "traditional" family. And since our family no longer "looked" the same—it no longer looked like the family we had been and had thought we were always going to be—I needed to change the "look."

She then describes how, talking and working with the children, this new vision was defined. The mission and vision she created outlined the values, principles, and other good things this woman wanted in life for her and her family. But simply having done this did not solve all the problems. As she started to act on the mission she had defined, she realized that

I had to come to a place with my personal feelings about the children's dad where I could value his goodness and still allow those things I didn't agree with. [At that time] I didn't want to forgive him. I didn't want to allow the children to go with him and do things with him. But my higher conscience, my better self, told me that that kind of attitude wasn't going to work in the end.

It wasn't easy. There were times when I was so angry I actually wanted to kill the man—especially when his choices kept hurting the children. But over the years I was able to work through my anger, and I finally reached the point where I could care for this man almost like a brother. I began to look at him not as my former husband, not as the father of my children, but as a man who had made some really tragic mistakes.

After talking about how each of the children also came to terms with their father and were able to redefine their relationships with them, she goes on to express appreciation for what defining a personal mission had done:

> What helped us most was in coming up with a new end in mind. We created a new vision of what our family would be.

As the preceding letter illustrates, a Personal Mission Statement need not be limited to individuals. A family can also have a unifying sense of mission based on what is important to its members. Whether for you or for your family, the important thing is to have such a guiding declaration.

Before moving on, I can't emphasize enough the importance of taking the time to review carefully your own goals and governing values and to synthesize and identify your own personal and/or family mission statement. True, it may be difficult to identify what is truly important to you, but boiling it all down into your own Personal Mission Statement will give you a document that will become a standard against which all the competing activities and events of your life can be measured. It can be as powerful a document for you or your family as the preamble to the United States Constitution, the national mission statement, that has guided the American nation for more than two centuries.

Chapter 7

"The Greatest Force
in Creation . . ."

There is only one miracle, and it is already accomplished.
That miracle is the human soul.

—*Hermann Hagedorn*

The concept of the atom has fascinated me ever since high school chemistry and physics. First of all, an atom is so small that our optical instruments are not powerful enough to enable us to actually see one. Scientists now estimate that 10 million of them laid side by side would occupy only one millimeter (about four one-hundredths of an inch).

Then there's the idea that all atoms are made up of the same basic ingredients: positively charged protons, negatively charged electrons, and neutrons, which contain no electromagnetic charge. Protons and neutrons form the atom's nucleus, and the electrons circle in orbits around the nucleus. Keep in mind that none of this atomic structure or activity can be directly observed. Scientists have deduced our conception of atoms by observing the effects produced by various natural phenomena and by conducting experiments.

It's also interesting that these protons, electrons, and neutrons form the fundamental building blocks of all matter. Protons are all alike, electrons are identical, and neutrons likewise. Exactly how these building blocks combine to form atoms is still one of the mysteries that challenge scientists today. But when equal numbers of each are combined, the atoms create what chemists call the basic

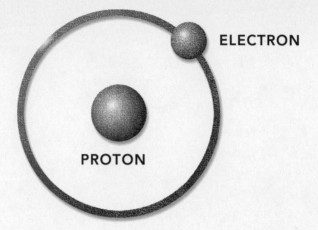

ELECTRON

PROTON

elements. Hydrogen, the simplest and most abundant of the elements, consists of one electron circling one proton, the only element that does not contain any neutrons.

Oxygen has a nucleus of eight protons and neutrons, circled by eight electrons. Uranium, one of the "heaviest" naturally occurring elements, consists of ninety-two protons and ninety-two neutrons, with ninety-two orbiting electrons.

I can't remember the point at which I was struck by the similarities between the structure of an atom and our solar system—the only difference being one of scale, from the unimaginably small to the equally unfathomably large.

If all these things had not been conclusively demonstrated by several centuries of science, it would be easy to dismiss the idea of atoms as little solar systems of charged particles as preposterous. Could one of the littlest building blocks of matter really have the same structure as one of the most immense? It is equally mind-boggling that man has learned how to harness the power that exists in the tiny atom. In nuclear fission, the process used in an atomic bomb, the nucleus of a uranium atom is bombarded with neutrons. When this happens, the nucleus splits, releasing more neutrons that can split additional uranium atoms; this sets up a chain reaction that releases tremendous amounts of energy. In nuclear fusion, the process at work in hydrogen bombs, the opposite process occurs. It involves a similar rearrangement of the protons and neutrons of an

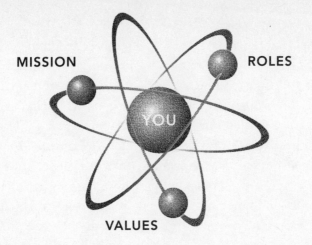

MISSION   ROLES

YOU

VALUES

atom. Physicists tell us that the fusion process releases even greater energy than the fission process and is the process that creates the light and energy of the sun and most of the other visible stars.

Why all this talk usually heard in a physics classroom? I wanted you to understand some of my excitement when I first realized that the tri-quation is really much like an atom. The nucleus of the atom is you as a physical, spiritual, and emotional being—a unique and individual creation. You contain unimaginable potential. The circling electrons are external things that help describe who and what you are. The first electron spinning around this nucleus with great speed represents the roles that we play. The second electron is the governing values we've identified that will help us perform within those roles. The third electron is the mission that we have discovered we are going to give our lives to. These three electrons represent what you have been identifying and clarifying in the past three chapters. When taken together, we have a dynamic atomic model that is a portrait of the real you. And like the atom, you have tremendous potential energy within that can be released.

So now the two-dimensional tri-quation has become a three-dimensional and powerful atomic unit: you. As you see this model go from a static example to a synergistic, powerful, energy-giving metaphor, I hope you can also see how this self-concept will give direction and power to your life.

While considering the metaphor of the atom, keep in mind that the power within you can be used for good or evil. The uranium or plutonium atom can generate electricity that will light cities and nations, but it can also provide the power to destroy those same cities and nations. As an example, the personal atomic reaction that Winston Churchill brought to the planet for good was magnificent. His adversary, Adolf Hitler, came to the planet and did a lot of evil. He used his power to destroy. It is important for us to realize that *we choose how we're going to harness and direct this power.* If we harness and direct it for good, miracles happen. If we harness and direct it for evil, destruction happens. There's a wonderful statement, "The power to lead is the power to mislead, and the power to mislead is the power to destroy." If you were to line up the ten most powerful public speakers in the twentieth century, Winston Churchill would clearly be one. So would Adolf Hitler.

An influential teacher in my young adult years once gave me an essay or poem (I've never been quite sure which way to categorize it) entitled "The Bomb That Fell on America," by Hermann Hagedorn. This is a beautifully written and powerful allegory in which a nuclear bomb has apparently just devastated the United States. One of the survivors has been dispatched to God seeking a miracle that will restore the people's faith in themselves and their ability to deal with their problem. After chiding him about asking for a miracle, an instant solution to the problem, God tells the messenger that "there is only one miracle" and it has already been accomplished in the human soul. "The soul is like the atom," the man is told. "Wonderfully like the atom. Consider the atom, so minute no lens you can make can enlarge it to a point where your eye can see it, yet there's a whole solar system inside it, whirling around a nucleus like the planets around the sun. So feeble in its unreleased state, yet actually the greatest force, save one, in creation. The greatest force in creation, save one. . . .

"I have given you a soul," the voice thunders, "and you ask me to come down and do a magician's trick!" After explaining how the people who discovered atomic energy had not begged him to come down and split the nucleus of the atom but had set to work on their own to do it and release the energy, he draws the analogy about how we can release the energy inside each of us:

> There is power in the human soul, when you break through
>   and set it free.
> Like the power of the atom, more powerful than the atom,
> It can control the atom, the only thing in the world that can.
> I told you that the atom is the greatest force in the world, save
>   one.
> That one is the human soul.

Every time I read these words I get goosebumps because they bring home once again how powerful the human soul is. That is why the nucleus of this personal atom that you've been discovering and defining is so important. It is more powerful than all the atoms in the universe. And when we surround that nucleus with clear definitions of who we are, what really matters most to us, where we're going and why, miracles begin to happen in our lives and in the lives of the people we serve.

It is my hope that I have helped you see the power of this atomic metaphor. If more people realized the atomic structure in their lives and allowed the power of who they really are to come forward into full consciousness, the positive energy released on the earth could make a difference that would be immeasurable.

Part Three

Doing Something About What Matters Most

Knowing is not enough; we must apply.
Willing is not enough; we must do.
Goethe

The idea is to make decisions and act on them—to decide what
is important to accomplish, to decide how something can best
be accomplished, to find time to work at it and to get it done.
Karen Kakascik

S EVERAL years ago I visited Egypt and walked around the great
pyramids at Giza. These truly magnificent structures are incredible
architectural marvels, and it's hard to believe that they were already
ancient in Roman times and that travelers viewed them then with awe
just as tourists do today.

These great stone pyramids, rising at the edge of the Nile Valley,
are impressive not just because of their bulk and simple geometric

beauty but because they have fulfilled the aspirations of those who built them more than 4,500 years ago. They were intended to stand forever as monuments to their builders' belief that the human soul would also go on forever.

It is amazing that those builders would select the pyramid, the most stable geometric form known, for use in vertical construction. In reading about pyramids, I was surprised to discover that the most important feature of a pyramid is not a part of the constructed monument but the natural bedrock on which it stands. Even the most stable geometric form will not stand unless it rests solidly on bedrock. The pyramid's great weight needs to be evenly supported. If any part of the pyramid rests on sand or soil or fractured rock, there will be a zone of weakness that could cause it to collapse. That's why the builders of these gigantic structures dug away the desert sand and built their pyramids on solid rock.

We might liken the solid rock on which the pyramids rest to the bedrock you have discovered in the past three chapters, the sure foundation of who you are and what matters most to you. And as you build on that solid foundation, you can make of your life a monument that truly reflects your personality and uniqueness.

The pyramids of Egypt were built by god-kings who sought to leave a legacy that would endure through the ages. Similarly, there is an almost universal yearning in all humans for some kind of immortality, something that will endure beyond their death. That universal motivation is behind much of what we have talked about, the yearning that tells us life should offer more than it sometimes does. That yearning also expresses itself in the desire many feel to leave a legacy, something others can look at to know that they lived and made a contribution. That's why each of us has such a sense of personal mission. It is almost as if we are genetically programmed that way.

If we're going to do something about personal missions and the things that matter most, we need to construct our lives with the same sort of meticulous care and architectural effort we would use to build any structure. Great lives and great legacies don't just happen. We must first prepare the plans, the blueprints, for the structure, and then we must follow them to a life that truly reflects who we are. We must manage the construction more seriously than perhaps anything else we do. To assist you, I will use our pyramid metaphor to illustrate the three major levels of developing your own Personal Productivity Pyramid, a way to represent the What Matters Most process as a pyramid built solidly on the foundation you have uncovered in the previous chapters.

As we look at the process of building the pyramid of your life, take heart in the fact that you have already uncovered the bedrock—you have *discovered* who you are and what matters most to you. This book has helped you dig deeply to uncover the foundation of your life's pyramid, representing the *why* of this whole effort. Now we'll extend the process to actually doing something about what matters most to you.

Chapter 8 will help you plan and develop your blueprints, describing both *what* you want to accomplish as well as *how* you are going to do it. Then in chapter 9 we'll talk about making it happen,

Personal Productivity Pyramid

the actual *act* of implementing your plans and turning them into reality.

In chapter 10 we look at how our behavior change is impacted by our individual Belief Windows. This powerful metaphor and tool will help you make sure that your perceptions of reality are actually in line with reality or things as they really are, not things as we wish they were or think they ought to be. Armed with your plan and a process for implementing it, you'll be on your way to bringing your life more fully in line with what matters most.

Chapter 8

Use the Inherent Power
in Planning

Failing to plan is a plan to fail.

—*Effie Jones*

 During the Vietnam conflict I had the opportunity of serving in the United States Army. I was drafted, went through Officers Candidate School at Fort Sill, Oklahoma, received a commission in the artillery, and found myself not in Vietnam but in Germany as a platoon commander for a Pershing missile unit. Pershing missiles are no longer part of the American military arsenal, but in the 1960s during the Cold War they were very effective short-range ground-to-ground nuclear weapons arrayed against the Soviet Union and its eastern European allies by the U.S. and NATO forces.

Germany has several Pershing missile sites, all looking eastward toward the Soviet Union in case there is ever a problem. Being placed in command of some of these missiles was a heady experience for a twenty-two-year-old. I had four warheads and missiles under my authority as a platoon commander. The smallest warhead our battery had was thirty-two times more powerful than the atomic bomb dropped on Hiroshima. I shudder to think about that now, but at the time it was just part of the job.

Because our mission was to keep these missiles in what was called readiness condition, we had frequent practice exercises where we would mock-fire them. Periodically we would simulate war exercises and take these missiles out to a field location, count them down to "T minus 2" (or two seconds before actual launch), stop the count, and then evaluate how well we had done in preparing the missiles for firing. If we had taken them the extra seconds, to "T minus 0," the missiles would actually fire. There were other safeguards in place to avoid an accidental nuclear disaster, but we were always acutely aware that the practice exercise countdown always needed to stop at "T minus 2" so as not to start World War III.

We had an experience one night in the middle of one of these war exercises that taught me a powerful lesson about preparation, planning, and knowing where one is going and what one needs to do in one's life. We had received a practice war message about 2 A.M., and I had to roust 150 men and have them get into their battle gear. The platoon was then to board their vehicles (there were more than fifty trucks, personnel carriers, and jeeps), go into the German countryside with five tracked vehicles carrying the nuclear weapons, find a predetermined location, erect our missiles, and mock-fire them.

We had with us from the group headquarters battery a warrant officer by the name of Chief Hewlett. I will never forget him and the lesson he taught me that night. Chief Hewlett had jumped into Normandy with the First Cavalry Division during World War II, had been in the Army his entire life, and had developed some real expertise in the Pershing missile system, which is how he came to receive his commission as a warrant officer.

For some reason, he was with our battery that night. We went out into the woods and started the process of putting the missile in place so we could fire it. When the missile got to a certain point in the sequence, we were to raise the missile off the launch vehicle and into the firing position, using a lift much like the one that raises the bed of a dump truck. When it reached the proper position, the missile would be seated on a big steel ring supported by three legs that could be hydraulically adjusted to compensate for uneven ground.

These legs were about 8 inches in diameter and very strong because they had to carry the entire weight of a missile that was 39 feet, or nearly three stories high. The warhead itself was about 11 feet long; the rest of the missile was made up largely of solid rocket fuel, similar to those that fire the boosters on the space shuttle. A small guidance and control section was located between the missile's fuel sections and the warhead. All together, a Pershing missile weighed thousands of pounds. When the missile settled down on its launch pad platform, in vertical firing position, it was critical that the three supporting legs maintain a level platform.

As we were going through the countdown, I was standing behind the missile with Chief Hewlett. At a certain point in the count the missile began to raise itself, going up from the horizontal position into a vertical launch position. The three legs of the steel ringlike platform had already gone to the ground and had leveled themselves. No sooner had the missile settled onto the platform than, for some unknown reason, one of the three legs retracted itself. This left the missile being supported by the remaining two legs, and just like removing one leg of a three-legged stool, the missile started to tip. It didn't fall over immediately because the platform launching ring on which it rested was still fastened to the launching mechanism and track vehicle.

It started to fall slowly. When this happened, an alarm went off to alert everybody that there was a very serious problem. Everyone rushed frantically to try to solve the problem. People were running here and there, trying to avert what looked like an imminent disaster. Visions of a court-martial or official inquiry flashed before my eyes.

One of our sergeants jumped to the malfunctioning leg and started to lower it down with a manual crank. That looked like a possible solution, but after he had cranked the handle about six times, I realized that he would not be able to get the leg down to where it would support the missile before it fell. Others were scurrying about frantically trying to discover what the problem was and how they could solve it.

As all of this flurry of activity unfolded, out of the corner of my eye I caught an unforgettable scene: Chief Hewlett, craggy-faced veteran of World War II and Korea, stood with his arms folded, his right hand under his chin, studying the missile. As the Pershing tipped ever more precariously, Chief Hewlett stood there for what seemed like an eternity but was probably only three or four seconds.

Suddenly, as if he had just experienced a revelation, he turned, dropped his arms to his side, walked toward the generators that were supplying power to the entire missile launch system, went to the back of the power units, and hit three switches in sequence. When he hit the third switch, the leg automatically went down very quickly and began to right the missile. It soon went back to the vertical position, and the problem was solved.

Everyone breathed a sigh of relief. What a few seconds before had looked like imminent disaster was now completely under control. I thought, "Holy cow! What happened?" The problem was solved. The disaster had been averted.

As the excitement died down, I walked up to Chief Hewlett and said, "Chief, what were you doing while you were standing there? What took you so long?"

His answer is one I will never forget: "Lieutenant, I had to plan what needed to be done."

I have reflected on that experience many, many times since. Chief Hewlett knew almost everything that could humanly be known about that missile and its associated systems. Somewhere in his brain he knew what had caused the problem and what was needed to solve it. He knew that running around and panicking was not going to solve it. So he stood there in complete serenity and solved the problem in his mind. Then he carried out his plan, solved the problem, and averted what could have been a dangerous situation.

There is a marvelous lesson in that experience for everyone, and it has to do with the importance of mentally creating before actually physically creating. We have to study things out in our mind. Whatever it is—a solution to a problem, a new business venture, a more harmonious family—it must be created in our brain first. When it has been created there and we have the vision of what must be done and what the end result will be, we can physically accomplish the vision in actuality. In the case of our tipping Pershing missile, it probably saved some lives. Because the launching exercise was a practice for the real thing, the warhead in the missile had not been armed, and there was no danger of a nuclear explosion. But Chief Hewlett's preparation and actions in the moment of crisis definitely saved millions of dollars of equipment and avoided injury or worse.

That experience with Chief Hewlett at 4 o'clock in the morning somewhere in the countryside of southern Germany exemplifies the definition of planning I have taught over the years. In order to do something about the things that matter most to you, it will help for you to understand a few basic principles about getting things done effectively.

For example, *planning is predetermining a course of events*—working through what must happen if a desired result is to be brought to pass. As you have progressed through the process of identifying what matters most, you most likely have a clearer vision of what those things are and what you want to do about them. The next step is effective planning, the key to making sure that you do something now about those things that matter most.

The only thing I would add to our definition that planning is predetermining a course of events are these two words: *in writing*. Why is writing important? Simply stated, writing your plan is vital to actually seeing it happen.

When I say that, people sometimes respond with statements like "But I get my best ideas in the shower" or "I do my planning when I'm driving in the car or out walking." What happens in the shower or in the car or on a walk can be a part of planning, but it's really only thinking about the project or activity. Unless it gets written down, you're like an architect trying to build a house without a set of blueprints. Until you produce a written plan, your profound thoughts too often will remain in the "someday" stage of development. A written plan, on the other hand, seems to produce a power and commitment that jump-starts the "doing" part of the effort.

Planning: Look at It Through Three Lenses

When you start developing your plans, it may be helpful to think of the planning process as a camera with three lens settings. On a point-and-shoot camera with a zoom lens, the wide-angle lens gives the big picture, the largest amount of visual information about the scene you are photographing. The close-up lens goes to the other extreme, showing the details of the scene up close. The mid-range lens offers a scene somewhere between the other two. Each lens has its

Camera Lens

purpose and advantages, and each provides its own particular perspective. In the big picture, we get a wonderful overview but can't make out any of the details. Likewise, in a picture with details, we don't see the larger scene. Sometimes it's good to have a view that provides some detail but also allows us to grasp some of the overall picture.

Applying this metaphor to planning how to do something about what matters most, the best place to start is with the wide-angle lens. You've already created much of this big picture view of who you are when you completed the exercises outlined in Part Two. At this point I hope you have a pretty good idea of the major roles you are filling in your life and that you also have a list of your governing values and a written Personal Mission Statement. These are the elements that provide the big picture of who you are and what's important to you.

Take a moment now and review. Start with your Personal Mission Statement, which will give you a very broad-brush picture of your purpose in life. Then look at the roles you are currently filling in life and the priority you have given each of those roles. Finally, read over your list of governing values and the clarifying statements you have written about each.

As you look over this panoramic view of who you are, select one of your roles to examine. This could be the role you currently feel is your most important, or it may be a role that you have been neglecting but feel strong urges to be more involved in. The choice of role is up to you. Write down that role so that you can keep it clearly before you as you move on through the planning process.

Now look at the governing values that arise out of or have a lot to do with this role, and write them down as well.

It is time to shift your view from the wide-angle lens to the mid-range lens. Take a moment to think ahead five or ten years or even longer and identify a long-range goal—something related to the role you have selected that you'd like to accomplish in that time period. What are some of the dreams you have about this role? Can you get one of them down on paper? In writing down your goal, put a realistic date or time period by which you think you can accomplish it. This can be very specific (March 25, 2005) or more general (within five years).

A Dream or a Goal

At this point we should probably talk about the difference between a dream and a goal. *A goal is a dream with a deadline.* Having a deadline on your dream will take it out of the limbo of "someday." The dream will acquire a life of its own, a time frame within which it will be accomplished. Your mind can envision its completion and how you will feel and how life will be different when its purposes have been implemented. The simple act of writing down a goal starts to unleash power and momentum that will help you see it accomplished.

At this point in the process you have accomplished two major pieces of the implementation process. You have determined *what you want to do* (the goal), and you have listed some of the *reasons that you want to do it* (the roles and governing values that are the motivations behind this goal).

The third and final piece of the goal-planning process is to determine *how you are going to do it*—the intermediate steps that will take you from here to there. This may seem like a fairly daunting task, but it's easier if you do a little brainstorming. When you think of something that has to be done to accomplish the goal, write it down. If your goal is to make a career change within the next two years, the intermediate steps might include such things as determining the kind of work you would rather do, identifying the skills that would be needed in your desired career field, finding companies or organizations that might employ you, and so on.

At this stage don't worry about the order of the steps. You can deal with that later. What you are trying to do now is think through the process of accomplishing your goal and identify the major steps needed to see it accomplished. Write down all steps, even those that seem way out or strange. The important thing when brainstorming is to put all ideas and thoughts on the table before evaluating them for relevance and fit. Later in the process you can strike out any that don't really apply.

When you think you have identified all the intermediate steps needed, determine the order in which they should be done. Identify the step that needs to be accomplished first, then identify the next step, and so on. The last thing you need to do is look at your list of steps and give each one a deadline. Be realistic as to how long it will take to do things, especially if your life seems to have too little discretionary time as it is. You don't want to have your long-range goals overwhelmed by the press of other events and responsibilities. If that happens, you'll probably get discouraged and give up before things can really get under way. The important thing is to *plan how you can do something about your goal on a regular basis*, with realistic intermediate deadlines that can serve as mileposts for your progress along the way. You may find that your final deadline is not realistic. That's okay. Unless there is some major reason that it can't be changed, set a new final deadline. In doing all this, you will find that the process has started you down the road toward achieving your goal.

Don't Be Afraid of the Power in Planning

One of the biggest reasons that we don't usually plan is the fear of commitment and its close cousin, fear of failure. It is okay to think about what we need to do to accomplish something, but if we make definite plans and put them on paper, we might fail. This fear of commitment and consequent failure is actually one of the strongest evidences of the power that preparing a written plan can bring to any endeavor. I know of no better way to succeed than to make a realistic plan and let that plan be the motivating force to carry it through to completion. Remember that the difference between a dream and a goal lies in writing your plan down. If you don't put it on paper, I can almost guarantee that you'll fail. Your goal will remain only a "someday" dream. You must now turn your plan into action.

Chapter 9

"Make It So!"

One can choose to go back toward safety or forward toward growth. Growth must be chosen again and again; fear must be overcome again and again.

—Abraham Maslow

 Somewhere in my early youth I was blessed or cursed (sometimes I'm not sure which) with a bias for action. Throughout my life I have generally found myself in a hurry to accomplish whatever I decided to accomplish, whether it is doing the yard work in half the time, getting my newspaper route done so that I could play basketball with my friends, or painting a fence in less time than everybody thought it could be done. "Getting it done" has always represented a kind of personal challenge, one that has served me well because I have been able to accomplish things.

In the early years of adulthood this bias for action carried over into my relatively short experience in the military. In the previous chapter I talked about learning the importance of careful planning in my experience with Chief Hewlett and the falling missile. Another such learning experience, this one dealing not just with planning but also carrying out plans, occurred while I was at Officers Candidate School at Fort Sill, Oklahoma, in 1966.

Those six months at OCS were designed to turn a young enlisted person into, in the Army's phrase, an officer and a gentleman. It was a grueling experience. Two-thirds of just about every class that went through OCS flunked out of the program and was sent back to the enlisted ranks prior to graduation. This was true with my class. We started with 180 officer candidates, but only 60 graduated. And it was with a feeling of great accomplishment that those of us remaining were graduated on December 17, 1966. We had somehow made it.

In OCS your rank was determined by your class standing. During my final weeks at the school I had the highest standing in the class and the rank of RINCO, or regimental commander.

Because of the influx of young men in OCS due to the growing problems in Southeast Asia at that time, there wasn't enough room in the old Robinson barracks at Fort Sill to house all the new candidates. One Friday morning the commandant of the school, Colonel Howard, called me into his office and said, "Candidate Smith, I have a challenge for you and your staff. We have more candidates here at OCS than we can house, and we're going to have to open up a part of Fort Sill that hasn't been used since World War II."

We got into his staff car and drove to an area that had been abandoned for years. It had three old wooden barracks with grass grown up around them about three to four feet high. No one had been in those barracks since 1945.

Colonel Howard said, "Candidate Smith, these barracks have to be prepared for an OCS class that will be here first thing Monday morning. Do you have any questions?"

I looked at the shambles and thought, "There is no way on this green earth that those barracks can be transformed into decent housing." Keep in mind that these buildings weren't even fit for prisoners of war, and the normal OCS standard was ten cuts above normal barracks. To have them OCS ready appeared to be a total impossibility. I looked at Colonel Howard, and the words that came out of my mouth stunned me: "Colonel Howard, it shall be done."

I then raced back to my office and met with six staff officers who also had their rank because of their standing in our class. I explained to them the challenge that we had been given. To a man they muttered obscenities and said there was no way it could be done. Then my bias for action kicked in, and I had the audacity to say, "Not only is there a way it can be done, but we're going to do it."

We sat down to plan how to accomplish the task. For the next several hours that Friday the seven of us worked on a plan to bring those barracks from dilapidation to OCS standards. We decided that we would need eight hundred men and three truckloads of cleaning and carpentry materials. We would need tile for the floors, new windowpanes for all the windows that had been broken out, and paint supplies. We would need buffers to clean and polish the new floors when they were in as well as new bathroom fixtures.

That was some list we created! We then called in the battalion commanders in the lower and middle part of the class and told them that at 1800 hours on Friday their battalions were to be in working clothes standing at attention in front of those barracks.

Three of my staff officers and I went to the supply depot at Fort Sill and presented the list of needed materials. The first sergeant looked at the list and laughed. He said there was no way in hell that we'd get all that stuff. I told him to call Colonel Howard and find out from him if we could have what we wanted. The first sergeant made the call and then said, "You've got it."

We filled three large army trucks with the materials, and at 1800 hours on Friday we pulled into the parking lot near the old barracks. Eight hundred men, led by their battalion commanders, marched in wearing their working fatigues. We split this wonderful force into about fifty working units, gave them their instructions, and at about 1830 the work began.

Between Friday at 1830 and Monday at 0600, a miracle took place at Fort Sill, Oklahoma. It was an exciting and magnificent thing to watch. The three-foot-high grass disappeared. Rocks materialized, neatly lined up all the way around each building. The rocks were then painted white. Gravel appeared where ugly terrain had been. All the old paint on the three two-story buildings disappeared and new paint was applied. The floors were all torn up and removed and new tile was placed. All the broken windowpanes, about three hundred, were replaced and new putty was applied. The old toilets, urinals, and mirrors in the latrines were replaced. The light fixtures were either fixed or replaced. The missing shingles on the roofs were all replaced.

By late Saturday night it had become clear that we were going to be able to pull this off, but it was also clear that no one would get any sleep. It was really a magnificent thing to behold—the camaraderie that occurred, the teamwork that took place, and the excitement as people saw the transformation and knew they were part of the effort.

One attribute of an OCS barracks was a floor that was so highly shined you could actually see your face in it. When the old linoleum tile came out and the new floor tile went in, seventy-five men in each barracks began to wax and shine those floors. This was the last thing we did. We started that final task late Sunday night so that when Colonel Howard and his staff walked in the next morning, we wanted them to see their faces in the floor just as in any of the other OCS barracks.

At about 0400 on Monday, the task was finally complete. Eight hundred tired men lined up in the parking lot of what was now a beautiful area. You would have thought golf course groundskeepers had maintained the area. There wasn't a blade of grass out of place. There wasn't a rock out of place. There was new paint everywhere. The place literally glowed. All the lights were on. All the bunks were inspection ready with fresh linen, and you could bounce a quarter off any of the taut blankets on the bunks. The bunks and the new foot lockers were lined up meticulously to form perfect rows. The clothes hangers that would soon hold the uniforms of the new OCS class were lined up two fingers apart in every wardrobe cubicle in three entire barracks. As an extra touch, we plugged up the new urinals, filled them with water, and actually put goldfish in them so the new men would be greeted with a touch of humor in their immaculate new latrines. It really was a sight to behold.

I told the men they could return to their own barracks but to be back in their Class A uniforms at 0600 hours to receive Colonel Howard and his staff. This way they could see the officers' reaction to what the group had accomplished. The battalion commanders gave the men their orders, and they jogged in formation back to their barracks—having had little or no sleep for sixty hours.

My staff and I returned to our barracks, took showers, put on fresh uniforms, and went back to the area just before the rest of the group. At 0600 hours, eight hundred candidates in their spanking clean uniforms marched back into the parking lot and stood at attention in front of the transformed buildings. It was still dark. We turned on all the lights in the buildings.

At 0605, Colonel Howard and three members of his staff, all majors and colonels, drove into the parking lot. I'll never forget what Colonel Howard said after stepping out of his car and looking at the three barracks that glowed in the early morning light. He walked over to where I was standing. I saluted him smartly, and he said, "Oh my God, I don't believe this." That was worth the entire sixty hours of effort. My staff and I then followed Colonel Howard and his staff through every building, on both floors of all three. We walked around the outside as well. The whole tour took about thirty minutes, as the 800 candidates stood at parade rest in the parking lot.

When we got back to his car, he looked at me and said, "When I gave you the challenge of getting these buildings ready, I thought there was no way that you could do it. I thought you'd have them just basically livable so that the new class coming in could take the next six months to get them ready. This is the most magnificent thing I have ever seen. How did you do it?"

I pointed to the men standing in the parking lot and said, "They're the ones who did it, sir. You need to tell them." He then walked out in front of all those men and spoke as loud as he could, expressing his astonishment at their magnificent accomplishment and saying again that he never dreamed in a million years the area would have been OCS ready in sixty hours. He again thanked everybody for a job well done, got back in his car, and left.

As those 800 candidates marched out of the parking lot and headed back to their mess halls to start another week at OCS, I looked back at those three barracks with emotion. We had done the impossible; we had accomplished what nobody believed could be done. We planned to do it, we knew we would do it, and we pulled it off. The satisfaction that came from that and the impact that this experience has had on my life has been immeasurable. Every time I am faced with a situation where people say it can't be done I remember again standing in front of those barracks realizing that we had accomplished the impossible.

"Make It So!"

I've always been impressed with the military command phrase used in the science fiction series *Star Trek*. When Captain Jean-Luc Picard of the Federation Star Ship *Enterprise* issues an order, he doesn't just say, "Do it!" or "My orders are to . . ." He says, "Make it so!" I especially like both the delegation of personal responsibility and the bias for action that is inherent in that phrase. You don't just do something in response to that command; you also take the responsibility to make it happen. I hope you'll keep that in mind as you now take a look at the plans you made in the previous chapter. We're going to talk about how you can "make it so!"

Your earlier work in identifying your roles, governing values, and personal mission has helped you build the foundation of your pyramid, to discover who you are and what matters most to you. I hope you have also developed a written plan for achieving one or more goals related to some of those things that matter most—the second level in the pyramid. Now it's time to move to the highest level of the pyramid and act on your plan—to schedule and carry out the steps that will be needed to see your goals fulfilled.

Much as you might wish it would, life won't stand still while you focus on accomplishing your plans for the things that matter most. You must integrate these new goals, tasks, and activities into the rest of the larger whirlwind of modern life, with all its varied and competing demands. For example, maybe you've made the decision and formulated your plan to write the great American novel. But unless money isn't a problem and you have a personal staff to handle the ordinary chores of living, you must still go to work, attend boring and interminable meetings, deal with interruptions, drive the kids to soccer games, take care of the house and yard, shop for food and other necessities, get the car washed and serviced, and do all the other necessary tasks that life requires.

The detailed mechanics of time management are not the focus of this book, but in order to be effective in carrying out the plans you have made, it will be helpful for you to understand a few fundamental principles that underlie effective use of time.

Understand the Difference Between Urgent and Important

A number of years ago I taught a seminar at Citibank in New York City in which I discussed the difference between urgent tasks and important tasks, and I decided to ask a question: "How many of you in this room feel as if you would like to do or ought to be doing more reading?" Every hand went up. Then I said, "Well, you've obviously placed a value on reading, but you're not doing as much as you would like. Why aren't you doing it?" The room became suddenly quiet. I had already made the point that when we tell someone we don't have time, what we're really saying is that we value something or some other event more, so no one was willing to say he didn't have enough time. I waited for a response. Finally a hand went up in the back of the room, and a gentleman in a very quiet voice said, "Books don't ring."

What a wonderful and true response that was. Who among us can resist the urge to answer a ringing telephone? But books don't jump up off your desk or your nightstand and say, "Hey, I'm a wonderful book. Why don't you read me?" Books just lie there. Until we have placed some urgency on reading or anything else, it tends not to happen.

In the process of actually doing something about what matters most, you must learn how to deal with all the other events and time-consuming things that will be thrown at you. Many of these will present themselves as urgencies—things you can't ignore and must address immediately: You have to file the tax return by April 15, and it's now April 14; you must stop what you're doing to help the son or daughter who has been hurt; the boss has just called and wants you in her office pronto; midterm exams loom in five days, and you still have four chapters to read; the phone rings with yet another telemarketer whom you can't seem to politely tell to buzz off. If your life is anything like mine, these competing pressures for some or all of your twenty-four hours probably sound familiar.

At the opposite end of the scale are the things that aren't screaming at us or forcing themselves upon us. Some of these may simply be attractive diversions that are "more fun" than other things we should do, or they are activities in which we engage almost by default, because we haven't planned anything else to do. They may be spending time in front of the television or playing a computer game instead of tackling a report. But some of the nonscreamers have a time dimension some distance out in the future and are overshadowed or pushed aside in our minds by the press of current events. Unfortunately, this is where we most often find our "Someday I'm going to . . ." dreams.

In order to deal with these competing priorities in the use of your finite time resources, you must decide the urgency as well as the importance of events and activities. For example, the looming tax deadline mentioned above would probably be both urgent and important, as would the need to help the hurt child and, most likely, the summons to report to the boss's office. But where would the telemarketer's call go? Unless it was Ed McMahon personally calling to announce that you had won the sweepstakes, it would probably be classified as urgent—if only because of the urgency of having to answer the phone—but not very important. Opening a mail sweepstakes solicitation would probably have neither urgency nor importance, along with most of couch potato time and other "by default" time-wasters. Studying for the midterm exam is important, but it may be urgent or nonurgent depending on how fast you can read or how well you feel you know the material now. Many factors will enter into the decision as to how to classify a particular event or activity, and the classification can change over time and may be completely different for each person.

While considering these classifications, you may find that many of the things that matter the most are important but not urgent. They are vitally important to us but are not screaming at us. Here is where most of our "someday" dreams are, along with relationship building, career or other preparation, and even doing many of the discovery exercises mentioned earlier in this book.

Unfortunately, the things that matter most are too often at the mercy of the things that matter least. Even among the things that are important, the nonurgent events and activities too often end up being bumped by the urgent ones. And to compound the problem, the important things too often get elbowed out by the nonimportant things, including almost all our personal time-wasters.

Perhaps what we've talked about here can be summed up in two key natural laws:

- Our priorities are the things that are truly important in our lives.
- Urgencies are not our true priorities; they act on our true priorities.

It is important to remember these two statements as you start to do something about the things that matter most. The urgencies, whether important or unimportant, will always be there, ready to divert you from the things that matter most. You'll have to do whatever is possible to protect your time and learn how and when to say no or how to gracefully move out of a time-wasting situation. *You will need to make time to work on your true priorities, including what matters most to you.*

And don't neglect an ongoing important but not urgent activity that can be one of your greatest helps in pursuing those things that matter most: your own personal preparation. This includes reviewing and updating the kinds of things that are discussed in much of this book as well as the need to regularly "sharpen the saw." This point is made by the old folk tale about a man who was so busy sawing wood that he couldn't take time to sharpen his saw. This, in turn, made it harder to cut the logs. In your planning, be sure to make time for reading, meditation, "smelling the roses," and regularly reviewing your roles, governing values, and Personal Mission Statement. From these you will derive a strength along with often-needed reminders as to what really is important to you in your life. To be effective in your efforts regarding what matters most to you, be sure to keep the saw sharp.

Place the Big Rocks First

Let me illustrate one fundamental principle that will help you make the most effective use of your time and efforts in doing something about what matters most. Perhaps you've seen the demonstration that I'm about to describe. It uses a large glass jar and other containers holding several large rocks and a number of pebbles. The challenge is to place all the rocks and pebbles in the glass jar. At first the

task appears impossible. It looks as if there is too much stuff to fit in the jar. The person conducting the demonstration assures you that it really is possible. What's the trick?

Actually, there's no trick involved, just an understanding of some fundamental physics. The person doing the demonstration starts with the pebbles, and it soon becomes apparent that there won't be enough room for most of the larger rocks. The person then demonstrates, starting with the larger rocks, fitting them into the jar and then adding the pebbles. This requires careful placement of the initial pebbles and quite a bit of shaking in order to get the pebbles to fill in the pockets and spaces among the large rocks. In the end all the pebbles are in the jar.

I've seen this demonstration taken to two additional rounds of materials, using sand and water. What looks like a sizable quantity of sand is poured into the jar, which is again shaken so that the sand grains can fill in all the little spaces left among the large rocks and all the pebbles. You are amazed when all the sand has been put into the container. Then the demonstrator empties a good part of a pitcher of water into the jar, and you watch in wonder as the water fills in among the sand grains.

There's a principle at work here that can help you plan your time more effectively. We might call this principle Place the Big Rocks First.

The rocks and pebbles metaphor is helpful to remember as you seek to implement your own plans for doing something about what matters most. The glass jar is the time that is available to us in a typical week. The large rocks are the activities and events related to the things that matter most. The pebbles are all those little tasks and things that fill up our lives. The sand could represent the many ways we spend our waking time. The water might represent the time we are sleeping.

Use the Close-up Lens to Implement Your Plan

It's time to return to the camera metaphor described in the previous chapter and switch from the midrange to the close-up lens. In developing your plan, you used the wide-angle lens to select from the panorama of who you are to one of the roles you fill in life. Then you switched to the mid-range lens as you identified and planned long-range goals, important outcomes you wish to accomplish that are related to that role.

The close-up lens might be likened to looking at the more detailed view of the "now" of your life, viewed from the perspective of a single week. A week provides a good amount of time for the final steps needed to accomplish your goals. A week is small enough to enable you to get your arms around it, to see it all at once and work within its time constraints and opportunities. But it's not so small that you get lost in the microscopic details of individual days. So think of the coming week as your large jar, soon to be filled with everything that takes up the time available to you.

I suggest that you set aside a time each week for your planning time. In your weekly session you'll want to do the following:

1. Review What Matters Most. The first thing to do during this time is review your written roles, governing values, and Personal Mission Statement so that you can keep those things uppermost in your mind as you proceed.

2. Review your What Matters Most long-range goals. Look over the goals you have formulated and determine which of the intermediate steps could be addressed this week.

3. Select the goals and intermediate steps you want to work on this week. Here you're selecting and creating a list of the "big rocks"—the events or activities you want to make sure get in the jar for the coming week.

4. Schedule the events beyond your control. These would be the absolute "have-tos"—meetings, appointments, and other events or activities over which you have little or no control. Since you cannot change them, you need to know where they fall so that you can schedule around them.

5. Schedule the big rocks. These are the intermediate steps related to what matters most. You'll need to be sure they have a place in the jar. Waiting to see if there's any time left over before scheduling the big rocks will all but assure that they are pushed out of your week. Schedule the big rocks at the times you can best get them done or, in the case of multi-day tasks, at least make some significant progress. If necessary, make an appointment with yourself and block out the time so that it won't get filled up by some urgency that comes along later.

6. Schedule everything else. With the big rocks in place, you can now fit the pebbles in around them. If your schedule is busy, be sure to leave some breathing room, especially around the big rocks. Leave yourself some time to allow for the unexpected as well as time to sharpen your saw. A completely full schedule is a surefire stress producer. If all the pebbles can't fit in the jar, you will at least have made sure that the most important things are. Some of the pebbles may have to wait for another week. Also, there is value in *under*planning your days to allow for all the little and relatively unimportant things we all seem duty-bound to place on our task lists. Look at the blank places in your schedule as, in the words of one seminar participant, "time to be wisely invested to reach some personal goals."

Time Now to ACT

With your week planned, it's time to take action, to do things that will produce the results you desire. Remember that action always takes place in that dynamic moment of time we call *right now*. And it's in that moment we usually run into our biggest trouble. If we act in the moment by just reacting to the events and activities that come at us, we may find ourselves being accidentally productive. But we may also find ourselves simply being reactive and going around in circles, tossed to and fro by constantly changing winds. When we act on what we have identified as mattering most that day, we are more productive and have a greater feeling of accomplishment and productivity. And when we act on what really matters most that week, we experience ultimate productivity and a feeling of fulfillment and inner peace.

The secret to effective daily decisions and action is something I like to call *Laser Thinking*. In some ways it's like that childhood ritual most of us probably went through when we tried to burn things with a magnifying glass. Fortunately, the incredible power of the sun is diffused in its normal state so that we don't get burned every time we walk outside. The magnifying glass focuses those rays to the point where the concentrated energy can burn paper or other things.

What I'm suggesting is that we all have tremendous power within us. The trouble is that most of the time that power lacks focus. And what we do in the moment of choice will also lack focus unless we are absolutely clear about what matters most to us and what we are going to do about it. When we have that clarity of personal vision, we bring the energy together just like a magnifying glass or a laser does with light. With Laser Thinking in the moment of decision, you will be able to see through the fog and cut through all the clutter to see which events and activities will further what matters most to you on any given day and which events and activities are just filler.

Most of the great thinkers and heroes of our lives have the ability to use Laser Thinking. This ability enabled Winston Churchill to cut through the political fog that encompassed so many of Europe's leaders in the dark days of German rearmament and the mortal perils of World War II. We've seen Laser Thinking at work in world-class athletes such as Michael Jordan whose incredible focus seemed to enable him to will a game to be won when the chips were down. It all begins with understanding who we really are and what matters most to us. Armed with that kind of self-vision, we can bring Laser Thinking to bear on the decisions we must make in our moments of choice. One such moment was shared recently by one of our seminar participants. Referring to his determination to balance his work needs with a passion to do something about improving his music skills, he wrote:

There is incredible peace of mind from knowing that information [about my priorities and schedule] will not be misplaced, and also peace from knowing that if something can't be done today, it won't fall through the cracks. I also feel truer to myself, knowing that my goals and dreams are always with me. I've always been successful, but now feel more in charge of my life.

I've been doing software engineering by day and seriously practicing electric bass at night. Before, fiercely determined to not give up the music, I might find myself practicing very late at night and not getting enough sleep. Now, I admittedly still might end up doing that, but less often, and also I am consistently getting a bigger chunk of time in which to practice the music: the time that I really want to spend on it in order to become the player I will one day be. I still have to work on understanding just how many things can be done in one day, but that is just refining the technique and will come with time. Right now, it is simply good to feel less like I've got the tiger by the tail, and more like I'm riding the tiger!

Fighting Our Demons

I wish I could say that doing something about what matters most is just as simple as following the principles I've outlined in this chapter. Unfortunately, you'll still need to find ways to deal with unwanted telephone callers, folks who poke their heads into your office to share the latest gossip, and the unplanned-for emergencies at work, home, and elsewhere. There may still be times when even your new and clearer personal vision of who you are will not be sufficient to motivate you to do something about what matters most.

An interesting phenomenon takes place in most people's lives when they decide to accomplish something important. The decision may be little or big: to go back to school, to change jobs, or to accomplish some big task at work. After making those decisions, we often experience a battle with what I call our demons. It's almost as if little devils sit on our shoulders and speak words of discouragement and defeatism into our ears. These demons seem to dispense all the reasons for your not doing what you've just decided to do.

There was a time when I had gained some weight that I didn't want, and I decided to lose it. At first I got pretty motivated about it: "Gee, I've got to lose twenty-five pounds, and I'm really going to do this." But within nanoseconds after making that decision came the demons: *There's no way you're going to lose that weight. You have to exercise, and you hate exercise.* These inner voices tried to convince me that I couldn't do it. We have to deal with these kinds of inner demons throughout our lives, and if we're going to whip them, we must not allow them to be successful in their quest to stop or derail us.

The most effective tool I have discovered in whipping the demons is to have regular victories in my life every single day. When you do something right, take a moment and savor the feeling. Even a little victory does wonders for your confidence and motivation. Make a conscious effort to successfully complete some task each day related to something that really matters to you. That'll help keep the demons at bay.

Fear of Failure

There are many types of diseases that afflict the human body, and we spend millions and perhaps billions of dollars trying to find cures. But there is one disease of epidemic proportions in our society on which we spend little or no money or effort—the crippling disease called fear of failure.

When my oldest son was a junior in high school, he competed for and won a position on the basketball team. He was very excited about being able to play for his high school. In the first part of the season I noted some interesting behavior during his games. When he shot a ball and missed, he didn't shoot for the rest of the game. If he ran into one of the opposing team players, he backed off. He stopped being aggressive and stopped going after the ball. This pattern was repeated off the basketball court. If he got bad grades in school, he became very difficult to be around and turned inward; he even got ugly on occasion because of my reaction to his grades.

Being a concerned parent, I confronted him on one occasion and asked him why he stopped shooting, why he backed off when he ran into one of the opposing players, why he got so ugly when he got bad grades. I didn't get my answer immediately. We talked about it for some time, but finally, in a moment of total openness, he mentioned that he was deathly afraid of failing.

A big red flag went up when I heard him say that, and I said, "I think we finally found the root cause of the problem. You have a belief that failure is bad. Where did you get an idea like that?"

In a trembling voice he said, "Dad, you don't know anything about failure."

Surprised, I said, "What do you mean I don't know anything about failure?"

He responded, "Come on, Dad. You have this big company. All these people work for you. What do you know about failure?"

This exchange was followed by my describing to my son the failures that I had experienced in my life, and we resolved together that there was really nothing wrong with failure. It was part of the learning process, and the point was to get back on course after messing up.

One of the biggest things that keeps people from achieving what matters most to them is this kind of fear: *Suppose I really identify what matters most to me. Then I'll have to come face to face with what I'm not doing about what matters most to me, and I may see that as failure and I don't want to fail. I don't want to go through the ugly feelings that failure can sometimes bring. Therefore, I won't take the time to sit down and go through any of this stuff because knowing what matters most to me is going to open up the possibility of failing.* Fear like that can extinguish the human spirit. Don't let it immobilize you in your quest to do something about the things that matter most to you.

When we ended our conversation about failure that day, my son and I decided that there was a better and truer principle that he could believe in: Failure is part of growth and is how we learn. Armed with that principle, my son was a completely different basketball player. There were games when I thought he was too aggressive. He lost his surliness about getting bad grades. His failures were now learning experiences.

Closely related to the fear of failure is the fear of change: *Maybe I'm not totally happy, but at least I'm comfortable. If I do all these things this book talks about, my life might have to change, pushing me out of my comfort zone and sending me into unknown territory.*

In his wonderfully motivating book *Release Your Brakes*, James Newman talks about comfort zones, those places and conditions we gravitate to by the paths of least resistance, usually by default. Leaving our comfort zones can be difficult unless, as Newman counsels, we realize that doing so can be an adventure, a rejuvenating and exhilarating experience.

If we can consider leaving comfort zones as adventures, then we won't be afraid to fail and can understand that we might fail many times before we eventually succeed. Thomas Edison failed a number of times before he achieved some of his most important inventions, including the electric lightbulb. Mark McGwire and Sammy Sosa struck out more times than they ever hit home runs, but a person never hits a home run without taking a very healthy swing at the ball. And today no one remembers Babe Ruth's strikeouts. Remember, failing is nothing more than a lesson for the next and greater battle.

There is a wonderful story about a very successful entrepreneur who was asked why he was so successful. His response was "Good decisions." The second question was "Well, how do you make good decisions?" The response: "Experience." And then the final question: "How do you get experience?" And the response: "Bad decisions."

That's a wonderful treatise on how we grow. We learn by our experience. We learn by mistakes. We learn by failing. We learn by attempting something. Sometimes it works and sometimes it doesn't, but we find the better way. Do whatever it takes to get the fear of failure out of your system. Failure is a marvelous, magnificent blessing that teaches us how to grow.

This chapter and this book are not about failing but about succeeding. The processes and principles we've talked about are powerful and proven tools that will help you identify what you want to do and how to do it. Over the past two decades these concepts have made a major difference in my personal effectiveness and self-esteem. I've also seen them at work in the lives of thousands I have taught. They can do the same for you if you use them to live in accordance with what matters most in your life.

Chapter 10

What's on Your Belief Window?

We don't see things as they are, we see things as we are.

—*Anaïs Nin*

As the happiness or real good of men consists in right action, and right action cannot be produced without right opinion, it behooves, above all things in this world, to take care that our own opinion of things be according to the nature of things.

—*Benjamin Franklin*

Let's say that you've identified and clarified what matters most to you, and you've formulated some specific plans on how to implement those deeply held values more fully in your life. You may already have started to make those plans happen. But even after following the process, you may have found that you're not yet living happily ever after, that changing some of the long-standing negative behaviors is still difficult to achieve.

So what's the catch? What went wrong? Let me introduce you to your Belief Window. Like most people, you may not be aware of this little-known but highly important part of your person that affects many of the decisions you make and how you behave in different situations.

You cannot actually see your Belief Window because it's invisible, but we all have one. It is figuratively attached to your head and hangs in front of your face. Every time you move, that window goes with you. You look at the world through it, and what you see is filtered back to you through it.

Your Belief Window is always with you, filtering what you see—the oceans of data and information through which you must navigate each day—and helping you make sense of the world around you. It influences the way you perceive others, the way you read situations, and the feelings you have about yourself. And if there is information you do not wish to "see" or acknowledge, you use your Belief Window to filter it out and keep it away from you.

The tricky thing about the Belief Window is that you have placed perceptions on it which you believe are absolutely true, whether they reflect reality or not. For example, your experiences and social feedback may have caused you to believe that you are smart, stupid, beautiful, ugly, competent, incompetent, creative, or dull—regardless of whether they are true. And because you believe them, you unquestioningly act as though they are.

As you can see, the Belief Window exerts a powerful influence on our actions and behavior. That's why changing our behavior is sometimes such a difficult task. Even though we know intellectually that a certain behavior, such as smoking, is detrimental, a strongly held belief such as "It won't happen to me" will keep us from making the necessary changes in our life. Erroneous perceptions on our Belief Windows can be a major detriment to our efforts to get our actions more consistent with our most deeply held values.

Until we realize that we view the world through our Belief Windows and that it constantly filters our experiences, we will continue to think that we see life "as it really is." But unless our Belief Window truly reflects reality—things as they really are, not as we wish they were or think they should be—we find that we can easily fool ourselves and potentially damage our chances for success in any activity we undertake.

One of the most important things we can do is make sure our Belief Window is as clear as possible and truly reflects what is happening in our life. This may be the most difficult thing I have asked you to do. You will probably have to swallow your pride, and admit that you do have a Belief Window that affects much of what you do, and recognize that some of the things you've placed on it are incorrect. In doing so you will have achieved the critical first step in freeing yourself from erroneous self-ideas and self-talk that may be impeding your progress.

What Is Written on Your Belief Window?

On our individual Belief Windows we have placed all the things we consider true about the patterns we see in the world, ourselves, and those around us. They might be as simple and as obvious as: "Objects will fall to the ground when dropped from the top of a building" and "Antibiotics kill bacteria that cause infections." These beliefs are based on scientific evidence and testing and thus could be considered "correct" beliefs. A belief such as "Women are more compassionate than men" may be less absolute but still generally true, based on experience. A belief such as "The world is flat," once widely held, has been proven to be incorrect or untrue. Sometimes our beliefs accurately reflect reality; sometimes they do not. Some of our beliefs may be completely subjective. But regardless of whether they are true or not, we believe them to be true and we will act as if they are.

Everyone has a mix of correct, incorrect, and debatable beliefs on their Belief Window. All of them influence behavior. Remember, the terms "correct" and "incorrect" are not moral judgments. If a belief reflects natural law or reality, it is considered "correct." If it's not rooted in reality and hence just doesn't work, it is considered "incorrect." A belief that is a subjective judgment or a matter of opinion is neither correct nor incorrect. In all cases, though, the key is to identify the beliefs on our Belief Window and change those that are incorrect or inadequate.

Testing Your Beliefs

We can perform tests on our beliefs—either actively or through observation—to see if they are true, false, or just matters of opinion. Scientists are in the business of testing beliefs (called hypotheses or theories), and through their efforts the world has replaced many incorrect beliefs with correct ones. But the problem with our personal beliefs is that we do not necessarily know whether they truly describe reality or are just misconceptions on our part. Our lack of testing can cause trouble for us because we conduct our lives as if everything written on our window is true.

In addition to a personal Belief Window we sometimes acquire what might be called a collective Belief Window. This window is filled with beliefs we pick up in collective settings, such as the organization we work for or groups to which we belong. When we look through these two windows at the same time, we may find that the beliefs on one sometimes conflict with those on the other, and then we have to choose which window has higher priority. The culture of the organization where you work, for instance, represents a collective Belief Window, and on that window you may find a belief that insists on a high degree of conformity among employees. If your own Belief Window says, "Individuality and creativity are important," then you will have to choose which belief to follow. If you choose to conform, you may find yourself highly frustrated. If you choose to express your individuality at work, you may be branded a maverick and be overlooked for promotions and raises because you aren't a "good corporate citizen." Perhaps, by recognizing these two Belief Windows and the conflicting things on them, you may choose to find new employment, where the collective window is more in harmony with your personal beliefs.

Belief Windows Define Our Limits and Set Our Capabilities

The beliefs on our windows set parameters for our success and happiness. Anyone who has attended a hypnotist show has seen how dramatically this principle can work. A friend told me about his experience at one such show where a small man volunteered to be hypnotized. Before the hypnotist put him under, he asked the man to sing something. His voice was raspy, and he hesitantly got through the song even with the laughter of the crowd. Clearly written on this man's Belief Window was the idea "I cannot sing."

But then that belief changed. The man was put under by the hypnotist and quietly told he was a world-famous singer about to give one of his finest performances. He was standing before a huge audience who had paid over $20 each just to hear him. He was then asked to sing again. The difference was dramatic. This time he was quite good and very pleasing to listen to—not $20 worth but still much better than the audience had expected. The only change was what was on this man's Belief Window. The perception the hypnotist had temporarily placed on it redefined his limits and his capabilities. When the temporary perception was removed, the man's self-defined limits and capabilities returned to their previous levels.

Your Belief Window Influences Your Actions

We place many of our beliefs on our windows as part of our attempts to meet our basic human needs, such as our need to live, to love and be loved, to have variety in our lives, to feel important, and to find meaning in our lives and existence.

For each belief on your window you subconsciously create mental rules that govern your behavior. These rules are "if-then" statements that translate your beliefs into actions. If you believe, for example, that "all Doberman pinscher dogs are vicious" (a belief clearly related to the basic need to live), your mind goes to work and establishes rules that will govern your behavior regarding Dobermans. More often than not, these rules exist only at a subconscious level, but they do exist.

A mental rule stemming from this belief might look something like this: "If all Doberman pinschers are vicious, then when I come upon a Doberman walking around unchained, I'll leap tall buildings with a single bound. I'll get away, run, evade. And I'll do the same thing every time." Another rule might be: "If all Doberman pinschers are vicious, then I will never own a Doberman pinscher. I will buy a St. Bernard or a Pekingese or a poodle or anything else instead."

You should understand that all this mental interaction about needs, beliefs, and rules is usually going on inside your mind where nobody can see what's happening, not even you. These thought processes operate at the subconscious level so that we are able to act automatically whenever we find ourselves in dangerous situations.

As we translate our beliefs into mental rules and then start to turn them into action, the workings of the process start to become visible.

To illustrate, let's return to the belief, "All Doberman pinschers are vicious." If you walk into my yard with that written on your Belief Window and I have a big Doberman running around loose, what are you going to do? Well, the rule you set up will automatically take charge of your behavior. You will jump the fence, climb a tree, or rush back out and close the gate. If you really need to see me, you may go to your car, call me on the cell phone, or retrieve some kind of weapon and approach the house like a soldier behind enemy lines.

Results and Feedback

What are the results of your behavior? And, more important, will those results meet your needs? If the results of your behavior do meet your needs, you could say that you have a correct perception on your Belief Window. If they do not, this suggests that you should take a closer look at both your needs and the belief you are using to try to satisfy them. But how do you really know whether or not your needs are being met by a certain belief? Well, the only way you can know for sure is to put the behavior to the test of time. Results often take time to measure. For example, if you spend years and years avoiding Doberman pinschers and never get attacked by one, you may conclude that your belief is correct. At least it's true that your need to stay alive and remain safe is being met.

Sometimes, though, safety is not our highest priority. Perhaps one of our other needs exerts itself and takes precedence over the need to live. Then we have a conflict. Suppose, for instance, that you have "All Doberman pinschers are vicious" on your Belief Window but it shares space with another belief: "Macho guys aren't afraid of dogs." Such a belief might derive from the need to feel important. But these two beliefs are in conflict. You can't follow both of them. In this case, you prioritize subconsciously and give higher value to one of the beliefs. If feeling macho is more important to you than feeling safe, you may be a bit uneasy around Dobermans but won't avoid them. You'll swagger past them, pretending to ignore them. And you may get attacked. That's the price you pay for giving more value to the belief that has the higher priority. And getting attacked may convince you to change a belief. You may erase "Macho guys aren't

afraid of Doberman pinschers" from your Belief Window and replace it with "Smart guys are afraid of Doberman pinschers."

The process of amending our beliefs happens all the time. It's
called experience. Ben Franklin wrote, "Experience keeps a dear
school, but fools will learn in no other." As another writer put it,
"Good judgment comes from experience; experience comes from
poor judgment." Our experiences cause us to alter our beliefs, adopt
new ones, or give them a higher value.

Results Often Take Time to Measure

I've already suggested that if the results of your behavior meet your
needs, you probably have a correct belief. Conversely, if the results
do not meet your needs, you can be fairly sure the belief in question
is incorrect.

Let's put this to the test. Let's say you're late for an appointment
and hurrying to get there. If you believe that "a competent driver like
me can safely drive above the speed limit" and you do indeed drive
that fast at times, does this mean the belief is correct? Well, not necessarily. You see, results often take time to measure. If we touch
something hot, we will know the results immediately. But the results
of many other actions may take years to become evident.

But what if you followed that belief your whole life and have
never had an accident, never even got a ticket? Is it a correct belief?
Again, not necessarily. Sometimes when we're operating on an incorrect assumption, we're lucky and manage to beat the odds. For
this reason it is often wise to perform two tests on some of our beliefs—one through our own experiences and one through the experiences of others. In this particular case we could look at data
regarding fast drivers—perhaps statistics about the average speed of
drivers involved in traffic accidents or drivers who ended up as traffic fatalities. Maybe statistics about the frequency of accidents for
both speeders and nonspeeders would be relevant. Or we might
consider the impact of speeding tickets for driving 85 miles per hour
on such things as driving records and insurance premiums. It is possible that common sense or potential bad results are enough to cause

us to look for better beliefs. "Safety is more important than punctuality" might be a more reasonable alternative.

The idea that "the speed laws don't apply to me" also suggests other beliefs are at work. One of these may be "It's okay to leave late for appointments." "Being late for appointments is bad for business" might be another. Perhaps changing one of these other beliefs will make the speeding belief irrelevant. "Arriving late for an appointment isn't the end of the world" would be an example. Or perhaps "Leaving early for appointments is a must." Another might be "Not breaking the law is very important to me." Any of these on a Belief Window would eliminate the need to rationalize excessive speeding.

Growth Is the Process of Updating Your Belief Window

We might say personal growth is the process of challenging and updating what is on your Belief Window. The first step is accepting the possibility that some of the things on your window are wrong. The willingness to do this is a sign of maturity.

After I finished presenting a seminar to one of our major clients, a working mother, one of the company's human resource executives, approached me. She described the transformation that had taken place in her mind as we were discussing the whole subject of correct and incorrect beliefs. She told me about the belief she had been living with for a long time: "Good moms stay at home." Then she described the guilt feelings she had been dealing with on a daily basis and how this affected her performance as both an executive and a mother.

Her belief was incorrect, and she had realized this during the presentation. What about single mothers or mothers in two-income families who simply have to work to provide food, shelter, and clothing for their children? Are they "bad" mothers because they work? Of course not. There is no connection between "good mothers" and staying at home. You can work and be a good mother. Through the seminar this particular woman began to understand that her assumption that "good moms stay at home" was yielding very unsatisfactory results in her life, and she reevaluated it. Then she told me that she was replacing the old belief with a new one: "Good moms are there when their children need them." This new belief gave her the peace of mind to increase her effectiveness at work and to focus her attention on the needs of her children.

Using the Belief Window to Change Behavior

A number of years ago when we were first clarifying the concept of the Belief Window, I was sitting in my office when my phone rang. It was the U.S. Attorney for Utah. He said, "I'm sick and tired of locking up kids in this state for drug and alcohol abuse. I've decided to go to every high school in the state. We're going to put on a big assembly and teach these kids how to get control of their lives. I have the Utah Jazz basketball team willing to send a player with us each time. Will you come along and give a thirty- to forty-minute talk and teach these kids how to get control of their lives?"

Well, wanting to make a difference, I got pretty excited about that and said, "Count me in. Let's go for it."

In the next three years we went to 148 schools in Utah, twenty schools in neighboring states, and talked to more than 300,000 kids. In March of the second year of this effort, we went to a high school in one of the rural areas of southern Utah. On this particular day the U.S. Attorney was not able to go. He had to be in Washington for some reason, so he sent an assistant U.S. Attorney whom we'll call Sam. The Utah Jazz basketball team was out of town that week on a road trip, and was not able to send a player, so just Sam and I went.

We walked into this high school. The principal met us in the foyer and took us into his office, sat us down, and said, "You guys are used to talking to the whole student body, right?"

I nodded. "Yes, we usually talk to the whole student body."

The principal responded, "Well, I don't want you to talk to the whole student body. They're not the ones with the problem. I want you to talk to my druggies and alcoholics."

"You *know* who they are?" I asked.

He said, "Of course I know who they are."

I said, "Hey, we'll talk to anybody you want."

"Great."

He took us down to the band room. If you have teenagers or have ever been a teenager, you probably know what a band room in a high school looks like. It has a graduated floor, with chairs on the terraces that rise from the front of the class. There was only one door to the room. Sam and I walked through the door, went over to the side of the lower front area, sat down, and waited for the bell to ring.

When it did, the door opened and in came fifty of the hardest looking kids I had ever seen. Conjure up in your mind the gang members and other tough kids you can see in our high schools today. Fifty of them came. One had green hair that stood straight up. Some of them wore jewelry or chains. Many looked far older than their years.

They sat down, draping themselves across the chairs. They looked around to see if they recognized anyone, and when they did, the hostility in the room went off the charts. This was an ugly, hostile group of kids.

The principal came in and walked toward the front of the classroom. Before he could get to the middle of the room, a kid sitting somewhere in the center jumped up. (Watching the assembling kids, I had picked this particular kid out as the ringleader.) He had earrings in his face you would not believe, in places you would not believe.

He accosted the principal and said, "Hey! How come we're all in here anyway?"

The principal said, "Because you're all druggies and alcoholics, and these two guys are going to fix it!"

Now I will tell you, I have had some wonderful introductions but none quite like this one. It turned out that the principal's statement constituted the entire introduction! He turned around and walked out. He wasn't even going to be here. Sam and I looked at each other.

Sam is a wonderful guy. Putting people in jail is what he does for a living, and he's very good at it. Talking to young people was really not his thing, however, and this became evident very quickly. For some reason, after taking three or four steps toward the front of the room, Sam felt that he needed to look more like the audience, so he tore his jacket off, took off his tie, and threw them on a chair in the front row. Then he said, "I'll tell you what, folks. If I catch you deal-ing drugs, I will lock you up and throw the key away. Have you got that? I'll lock you up."

The kid who had accosted the principal jumped out of his chair a second time. "The heck you will, Jack! [He didn't say *heck*; I learned some new words that day.] We're under eighteen, man. We're mi-nors. You can't touch us. Two or three weeks in the detention center, we're back on the street. You can't touch us!"

Then the whole class shouted, almost in unison, "That's right, baby. You can't touch us!"

They were right, and Sam was done. He was supposed to talk for fifteen minutes but was finished in ninety seconds. He walked back, sat down next to me, folded his arms, and said, "You can have this mob."

I got up and walked in front of them. When I am talking to people, I often have wonderful conversations with myself, and this was no exception. As I took those three or four steps, I said to myself, "You know, Hyrum, there's no way this can get any worse." It got worse! When I got to the front of the room, I looked at a kid sitting just a lit-tle to my right—a long-haired kid draped across three chairs, shirt open to his navel. He had these funky glasses on with spirals in them. This kid was feeling no pain whatsoever.

For some reason I succumbed to an impulse to take this kid on. I said, "Well, it looks as if we have our class nerd here."

The kid jumped out of his chair, took off his glasses, and said, "I don't have to take that!"

I said, "That's right, you don't! Why don't you get out?"

He said, "Okay, I will." He stormed over to the door, turned around, swore at me—three words I had never heard before—and slammed the door. Immediately almost the entire class shouted, "Hey, let's get the guy with the suit!"

You need to understand that when we normally did these things in a high school, we would have 1,500 kids in a big auditorium. We would show a twelve-minute film about three kids that got messed up on drugs, and then the U.S. Attorney would get up and talk about the legal side of drugs. This was followed by Karl Malone or John

Stockton from the Utah Jazz basketball team talking about drugs and athletics. Then I would do a lighthearted thing on gaining control of your life and would teach the students a poem from Shakespeare.

But this time I was saying to myself, "You know what, Hyrum? If you try to teach these kids a Shakespeare poem, you'll be dead meat. Today will be your last day on the planet. You had better do something else."

Up to this time I had never tried to teach the concepts of the Belief Window and governing values to a group of normal young people, let alone this kind of group. We were just developing the concept, along with a simple tool we called the Reality Model that showed the relationships among our human needs, our beliefs, the mental rules we unconsciously form about those beliefs, the behavior that is produced, and the results of our behavior. But I began saying to myself, "You know what? These kids are going to learn about the Belief Window and the Reality Model if it kills me." At that point I wasn't sure it wouldn't.

By this time the kids were being just about as ugly as they could be. They were noisy, throwing stuff, and just being rude. I had to shout to be heard: "Now listen up! I came down here to teach you a model. It's called the Reality Model. I'm going to burn it into your brain before you walk out that door. I don't have a blackboard up here, so I need five volunteers. I'll pick the volunteers. You, get up here." I picked one hard-looking kid, dragged him up to the stage, and sat him in a chair. "You're my needs. Here are four human needs. Commit them to memory with the rest of the class: *to live, to love and be loved, to feel important*, and *to have variety in our lives*. Now give me one back."

At first he couldn't give me even one need back. I finally got him to mutter one. To be my Belief Window, I picked the kid who had been accosting everybody. It took me six minutes to get his real name. He gave me eleven wrong names before giving his real name: J.D.

Soon I had five kids sitting up there, each representing a piece of the model. Over the noise I tried to tell the kids how the model worked: "Okay. I'm going to give you a belief you might have on your Belief Window. You tell me the need driving that belief, and let's take it through the model. Here's the belief: 'My self-worth is dependent on being okay with my friends.' "

(Do you know any young people who have that belief on their Belief Window? Do you know any older people who have that belief on their Belief Window?)

I said, "Give me the human need driving that kind of belief."

A kid popped up over on the side and said, in a rather smart-aleck way, "To feel important?"

I said, "Yeah, probably that. Also, how about to be loved? Maybe there are two needs driving that." Then I said, "Let's take that belief through the model. If it's true that I'm not okay unless my friends say I'm okay and I go to a party and my friends offer me drugs and alcohol, what am I going to do?"

The whole class erupted with comments like "Hey, man, whaddya think? You're going to take it."

I responded with a question: "Will the results of that behavior meet your needs over time?" They had no idea what I was talking about.

So we started taking different beliefs that people might have about different things and ran them through the Reality Model. Twenty-five minutes into this, J.D., the kid playing my Belief Window on one of the chairs up front, figured out the model. He stood up and said in a confrontational way, "Okay, Hy-rum!" (The groups I usually teach don't address me that way.) The class went deadly quiet. You could almost hear them saying to themselves, "Hey, man. J.D.'s going to get the guy with the suit!"

J.D. said, "Let me tell you how stupid this model is. You just told us that if the results of our behavior don't meet our needs, there's an incorrect belief on our Belief Window. Right?"

"Right!" I said. I could see exactly where he was going, so I stopped him at this point and said, "Now wait a minute, J.D. Do you drink?"

"Yeah, I drink."

"How much do you drink?"

"Eight or ten beers a week, and get smashed on weekends."

"Do you get smashed every weekend?"

"Yes."

"Are you an alcoholic?"

"No way, man. You can't be an alcoholic drinking like that."

I said, "You just gave me one of the beliefs on your Belief Window."

"I did?"

"Yeah, you did. You just told me that you believed you could drink eight beers a week and get smashed on weekends and not be an alcoholic. You told me you believe that."

"So?"

"That's all, J.D. I just wanted to make sure you understood. Go ahead."

He said, as much to the class as to me, "Okay, Hyrum. That means if the results of our behavior *do* meet our needs, there's a *correct* belief on our Belief Window. Right?"

"Right!"

"Okay, Hyrum," he continued. "I have a belief on my Belief Window. [As he said this, I got excited because he was using the vocabulary of the model; he understood what I was trying to teach.] I don't care what those kids think about me. [That was a big lie. What those kids thought about him meant a lot, but he couldn't admit that.] The belief on my window is that drugs and alcohol are *fun*. And the need driving that: *variety*, baby! Let's take that through your stupid model. If that's true, then I set up my rules. I go to a party, and my friends offer me drugs and alcohol. I take them. Do the results of that meet my needs? You bet they do, man. When I take drugs and alcohol, I feel terrific. That means I've got a correct belief on my Belief Window, right?"

The room was silent. I said, "Right."

And he said in a surprised tone, "Right?"

"Yeah, right. But you forgot the second law, J.D. Results take time to measure. You don't know yet. You may feel good that night or over the weekend, but over time is that going to meet your needs?"

"Okay, okay, man," he said. "That means I take drugs and alcohol all my life and prove it, right?" Smart kid!

And I said, "Yeah, you can do that. That's the dumbest way to find out if you have a good belief on your Belief Window, but you can do that if you want."

"How else are you going to do it?"

"It's called seeds and fruits."

"What does that mean?"

"That means you take a look at the life of somebody else who took drugs and alcohol all his life and see if it really met his needs. Can we do that?"

"Yeah."

I said, "Okay, J.D. You give me one example." At this point we are nose to nose in front of the class. I am dripping wet, but they didn't know that. I kept my coat on. I said, "You give me one example of somebody who took drugs and alcohol all his life where it really met his needs. One example!"

Do you know the example he gave me? Elvis Presley. I said, "Presley? Where's Presley, for crying out loud?"

"Dead."

"How come?"

"OD'd on drugs."

"Did that meet his needs?"

J.D. sat down.

I addressed the class. "Give me another example." The second example they threw at me was Janis Joplin. I said, "Joplin, where's Joplin?"

"Dead."

"How come?"

"OD'd on drugs."

"Did that meet her needs?"

The third example—and I am not kidding—was John Belushi. They were thinking of famous people. I said, "Where's Belushi?"

"Dead."

"How come?"

"OD'd on drugs."

"Did that meet his needs?"

For the first time I had their undivided attention. I said, "Now listen, folks. I didn't come down here to tell you what belongs on your

Belief Window. It's none of my business. I came here to tell you that you have a Belief Window, you have the same basic needs I have, and every day you're putting beliefs on that window that you think are going to meet your needs." Then I asked them, "Are you mature enough to take that window off, put it on the table, and find out if those beliefs are correct?"

Remember the kid I told you about with the green hair? He was in the back row, and since it was a graduated floor, he was up higher than everybody else. This kid jumped out of his chair and said, "This is all a bunch of crap."

"What do you mean?"

"Who cares about this stupid model? Man, we're all going to be dead in ten years anyway."

"What do you mean you're going to be dead in ten years?"

"Yeah, we're going to blow ourselves up."

I said, "You just gave me a belief on your window."

"I did?"

"Yes, you did. You just told me you believe you will be dead in ten years." Then I asked, "How many of you believe that?" Forty-three hands went up. I said, "Let's take this through the model. 'We will all be dead in ten years.' If that's true, then we unconsciously create some rules about how that belief will affect our behavior, and it's time for you to perform in school. How are you going to perform in school?"

The kid sitting next to him jumps out of his chair. "Hey, man, this is the dumbest kid in school. He's flunking out."

I said, "Flunking out? Will the results of that behavior meet your needs over time? Suppose that you're not dead in ten years. Suppose that twelve years from today you're still alive. Who's going to buy the green dye for your hair?"

This was a very confrontational experience. The kid looked as if someone had hit him with a two-by-four. He stood there and said, "Well, that doesn't mean you don't try."

I said, "The heck it doesn't. Are you trying today? How are you doing today in school?"

The kid sitting next to him jumped up again. "This is the village idiot, man. He's flunking out."

Just then the bell rang. The principal came in, and he had no idea what had been going on. I said, "Well, I guess our time is up."

Two kids said, "No way, man. We're not done."

I said, "You're not done? You guys want some more?" Fifty hands went up. There followed an animated discussion with the principal. "We've got to have another hour!"

"Can't have another hour. It's lunchtime."

"Well, can't we come back after lunch?"

"I guess you can."

"What time?"

"Twelve-thirty. Be in your seats at twelve-thirty." The room cleared in thirty seconds.

At quarter after 12, sixty kids came back, with the ten newcomers looking worse than the first fifty. The five kids sitting in front were in their seats at ten minutes after twelve. They had their lunches in their laps, and they wanted those chairs. That was very interesting.

When the rest of the kids came back, much of the earlier hostility had gone out of the room. I wouldn't say we were friends or anything, but a lot of the hostility had gone, so I figured I could get away with something. First, I brought the ten up to speed who had missed the first class. Earlier I had made some very important statements: When you witness a pattern of behavior, you can tell what's on the Belief Window. You can, or at least you can come pretty close. Scarier than that, if you know what's on someone's Belief Window, you can predict with some accuracy behavior and, ultimately, the results of that behavior. This gives you a powerful tool for examining your own motivations and actions, and a good way in general to understand others around you.

After bringing the ten up to speed, I said, "Before you left I said that if you witness a pattern of behavior, you can tell what's on the Belief Window. Right?"

"Yeah, man, that's right."

"Okay. I'm up here witnessing a pattern of behavior." From the look on their faces, I knew they were thinking, "What are you talking about?"

I continued, "You people look terrible."

When I said that, the hostility returned really fast. "Look at you people. If you tried to run in the world I run in, you wouldn't last thirty seconds with that hair, those clothes, all the tattoos and body piercing."

They were really angry now, and I was less than composed myself. I was going to make sure they understood my point. I turned to one long-haired kid. "You, stand up." He stood up. "You're wearing long hair."

"So?"

"How long have you been wearing long hair?"

"Five years."

"That makes a pattern of behavior, right?"

"Yeah."

"Well, there must be something on your Belief Window that makes you wear long hair. I want to know what that is." This kid stood there for a full minute. Do you have any idea how long a minute is when you're wondering whether you're about to die? At the end of the minute this kid said, "It gets my father's attention." Which of his basic needs were not being met?

Please understand that when any of our basic needs are not being met, all of our energy automatically flows to meeting that need. We start putting beliefs on our window that we think will help us meet those needs. If we put a belief on our Belief Window that drives behavior which works short-term but destroys in the long term, will we continue the behavior? Yes, we will, or at least many of us will, unless we decide to recognize and take control of the needs and beliefs that are underlying that behavior.

At this point I knew I had to win back these kids. They were all mad at me. I said, "Now listen, guys. When I first walked in here today, you saw me throw a kid out, did you not?"

"Yeah."

"Well, that is a pattern of behavior, is it not?"

"Yeah."

"Maybe I have something on my Belief Window."

"Yeah, you think all long-haired kids are rotten."

I said, "I don't think I believe that, but let's suppose I do believe that. Let's put that on my Belief Window: All long-haired kids are rotten. If I believe that's true, then I set up my rules. I come to your school, and a long-haired kid gives me a hard time. What am I going to do?"

The whole class: "You're going to throw him out."

"Right. And I did throw him out. Will the results of my behavior meet my needs over time?"

Sixty heads in the room nodded. I said, "No, no, no! Is that kid here?"

"No."

"Is he going to come to this class again?"

"No."

"Is he going to speak to me again?"

"No."

"Is that meeting my needs?"

"No."

"So what does that say about me?"

A kid pops up: "You've got a screwed-up Belief Window, Hyrum." I was excited because they were using the model perfectly.

A young woman was sitting there, a hard-looking young woman. She looked to be much older than her years. I said, "Stand up." She stood up. "You're wearing acid-washed jeans."

"So?"

"Do you wear those very often?"

"Every day."

I said, "That makes that a pattern of behavior, right?"

"Yeah."

"Well, there must be something on your Belief Window that makes you wear acid-washed jeans. I want to know what that is."

"They're cool, that's why."

I said, "Who said they're cool?"

"They did."

What's on her Belief Window? *I'm not okay unless* they *say I am okay, and if they say acid-washed jeans, what am I going to do? I'm going to wear acid-washed jeans.* I said, "I'm not here to knock acid-washed jeans. I have a pair myself. There is a reason we're doing it."

"Yeah, man. That's right."

J.D. jumps out of the chair. By this time J.D. and I are pretty good friends. He says, "Okay, Hyrum. There are two things we've got to run through *our* model." He said "our" model. "First of all, what did you come here for? Why did you come to our school?"

I said, "Because I have a belief on my Belief Window."

"Yeah? What's the belief?"

Can you imagine my excitement when I realized they all understood now? We were communicating. *What's the belief?* I said, "Well, the belief on my window is I'm supposed to make a difference."

"What does that mean?"

"I don't know exactly. I heard Winston Churchill give a talk once, and he said he was going to make a difference—and that guy did make a difference. I decided then and there that Smith was going to make a difference, too. Let's take that through the model. Which of the needs we talked about would drive something like that?"

A kid pops up: "To feel important."

I said, "Yeah, probably. How about to love as well? And how about variety, guys? I came here to talk to a sick group like you. Variety, trust me." They laughed. "Let's take that through the model. If the U.S. Attorney then asks me to talk to you about drugs and alcohol, what am I going to do?"

The whole class: "Man, you're going to do it." A kid says, mimicking my words and delivery, "Well, Hyrum, is it meeting your needs?"

I said, "I don't know. Remember, it takes time to measure results. I don't know yet."

Another kid says, "Well, if some of us stop taking drugs and alcohol, would that make you feel better?"

I said, "Yeah, I'd feel terrific."

J.D. then said, "Okay, okay! I understand that, but here's the real thing." He started pacing back and forth in front of the room. "There's this girl, she's my friend. She is not my girlfriend." The class got deathly quiet. They all knew who he was talking about. "She's a cocaine addict and an alcoholic. Her parents are alcoholic and cocaine people; they are totally screwed up and beat her every day. She called me this morning and said she is going to kill herself. This girl is out there thinking about committing suicide. How are we going to keep this girl from killing herself? Hyrum?"

Everyone was looking at me. They expected a golden answer from the guy with the suit. I thought for a moment and said quietly, "I don't know."

"What do you mean you don't know?"

"How am I supposed to know?"

"You've got a suit! You're supposed to know." (Talk about a screwed-up Belief Window.)

I said, "Well, I don't know. Let's put what we do know through the model."

J.D. said, "Well, we know her behavior."

I said, "What's her behavior?"

"I told you, man. She's a cocaine addict and an alcoholic."

Then I said, "Will that behavior meet her needs over time?" At that moment I had the most electric teaching experience I had ever had. Sixty heads in that room moved back and forth: *No.*

I said, "You've got that right. What does that mean?"

"She's got a screwed-up Belief Window," one kid offered.

J.D. jumps up again, "If I go and tell her she's got a screwed-up Belief Window, she'll throw me out."

I said, "That's probably right, guys. It's deeper than that. There's a need not being met. Which of her needs aren't being met?"

A kid stood up. I'll never forget this kid: six-foot-four, with an Army field jacket, scruffy beard, long hair, and rings everywhere. He was glowing, almost as if he had just had a revelation. He said, "Nobody loves her."

I said, "Yeah, that's interesting. So what are we going to do about that?"

He looked at me as if I were a complete idiot, "We love her, dummy."

"Oh. How are we going to do that?"

These kids then came up with the most wonderful ideas on how they could show that girl they loved her. I said, "Do you think if her need started being met even just a little that we could start talking to her about beliefs on Belief Windows?"

"Yeah."

The bell rang. Time was really up. The principal came back in and ordered everybody out. He still had no idea what had gone on in the room. As the kids were filing out, J.D. walked up to me, got right in my face, and said, "Let me tell you something. I've been in drug and alcohol therapy for ten years." This is a sixteen-year-old kid. His brother had given him cocaine when he was six. He said, "I've been in jail four times. I've had every shrink in this state try to figure me out. But this is the first time anything made any sense to me."

I replied, "J.D., I'm going to tell you one more time. I did not come here to tell you what belongs on your Belief Window. That's none of my business. I came to tell you that you *have* a Belief Window. You have the same needs I have, and you're putting things on that Belief Window every day that you think are going to meet your needs. Are you man enough to take that window off, put it on the table, and find out if those beliefs are correct?"

J.D. straightened his shoulders and said, "Yeah, I am."

I got right in his face now and said, "I guess we'll see, won't we?"

There are two powerful things about this metaphor of the Belief Window. First, it places responsibility for behavior right smack on the individual where it belongs. I believe that there arrives a point in time when we must take total responsibility for our behavior. You can't blame it on the neighborhood anymore. You can't blame it on your genes. You can't blame it on the fact that you're from some hick town. You alone are responsible for your behavior. If that's true, what else are you totally responsible for? You are responsible for what stays on your Belief Window. The thing that separates you and me from the rest of the animal kingdom is that we can change our Belief Window.

The second powerful thing is that you can be very confrontive about attacking somebody's Belief Window because you're not attacking them personally. *I'm okay, Dad, right? Yeah, I love you a lot, kid, but you know what? You have one screwed-up Belief Window, and we're going to have to do surgery on it.* The Belief Window is a symbolic representation of what's going on, and if it's happening anyway, why not take control of it?

We all have needs. We all have Belief Windows. We have set up internal rules based on those beliefs, and these drive our behavior. The trouble is that we tend not to measure the results and ask the change-initiating question: *"Will the results of this behavior meet my needs over time?"*

One little footnote: The high school episode took place in the southern part of Utah in 1987. It was such a powerful and moving experience for me that I've shared this story with hundreds of audiences all over the world. I have told the story so many times that I began to ask myself, "That's such a wonderful story. Did it really happen the way I have been telling it, or am I, in Shakespeare's words, 'remembering with advantage'?" When a story is so good and has such impact, you worry that you might have embellished it in the telling.

Several years after that experience, I was asked to be the keynote speaker for Southern Utah University's annual antidrug week. The individual who introduced me that evening, Tom Jackson, had been the drug and alcohol specialist for the school district in which the experience took place. What I had forgotten was that this gentleman was in the room that day.

When Mr. Jackson introduced me that night, he didn't say anything about his involvement with me that day. I gave my address, using the story as the last part of it. As I returned to my seat, Mr. Jackson went to the microphone and said to the several thousand students assembled, "I want you to know, ladies and gentlemen, that I was in the room that day when Mr. Smith had that experience." My chest tightened a bit as he made that statement. The thought raced through my mind, "Oh, no! I'm going to be exposed. I'm going to find out that it didn't happen the way I've been telling it."

He went on to say: "I want you to know that it is exactly what happened. I was in the room. I watched it happen." Gratitude and other emotions flooded my system when I learned I had been telling it as it had really happened.

That night Mr. Jackson also gave me an update on J.D. I was very pleased to find out that he had followed through with his resolve to graduate from high school and go on to college. The last time I heard about J.D. he had been mature enough to replace some of his inappropriate beliefs with ones that are serving him much better. For the group as a whole, there were two types of results. Ten of them totally turned their lives around as a result of discovering the Belief Window idea. Their behavior changed dramatically when they realized that what they were doing wasn't going to work for them over time. This didn't sink in for the rest of them in the room that day. For whatever reasons, the other forty or fifty didn't see a need to change, and so their behavior didn't change. But it was exciting and gratifying to know that ten people who had been headed for self-destruction were able to stand back, see what was happening to them, and make the changes needed to turn their lives around.

Your Belief Window can be a powerful force for shaping your life and your behavior in both positive and negative ways. It is especially important now as you find yourself earnestly striving to achieve congruency and harmony between how you are living your life and what really matters most to you. As you implement your plans to make new and better things happen in your life, be aware that you do have a Belief Window and that the perceptions you have placed on it, whether in line with reality or not, will either help or hinder you in your efforts.

Take the time to examine closely what is on your Belief Window. If you find beliefs or perceptions that are hindering you and holding you back, remember that they can be changed for beliefs that will serve you better. The closer your belief and perceptions are to reality, to things as they really are, the more successful you will be in meeting life's challenges and in living in accordance with what matters most.

Part Four

What Matters Most— the Broader View

It is good to have an end to journey toward, but it is the
journey that matters in the end.

Ursula K. LeGuin

At this point you have probably realized that fully implementing this process can take some time, especially in the area of doing something about what matters most. Indeed, living in accordance with what matters most will be a lifetime endeavor, but one with rewards and inner peace. Take heart in the realization that the hard part is done. Your roles and governing values have been identified, and your Personal Mission Statement has been written. You can now tackle as many or as few of your long-range goals as you want to take on at this time. There may be times ahead when things that are both urgent and important will press in, temporarily keeping you from focusing on what matters most. Just remember that the process is always there, waiting for you to use it whenever and as often as you desire.

Now that you understand the process and have participated in it, I'd like to explore some of the broader implications of what we've talked about. In chapter 11 we'll take a look at how the process and the principles behind it apply to businesses and organizations as well as individuals. In fact, the most successful organizations, those that have been successful for decades and even centuries, have followed the principles we've talked about. These "visionary" companies or organizations know who they really are and what makes them tick. And like the most successful and fulfilled individuals, they operate in accordance with what matters most to them in a business or organizational sense.

In chapter 12 we'll look at What Matters Most in terms of your influence in a wider circle, with special emphasis on how history and lives are most often changed by the efforts of single individuals—people who are armed with the knowledge of who they are, what matters most to them, and what their personal mission is. Such individuals have brought about major changes in venues as small as an individual family or community and as big as nations and even civilization as a whole.

Chapter 13 puts the What Matters Most process into a larger, lifetime perspective, and we'll talk about the idea that life isn't set in concrete. The relationships, events, and priorities of your life change over time, and what matters most to you will also change. We will look at some of those realities and the way the principles and process we've talked about can help you cope with the inevitability of change.

Finally, in chapter 14, I'll share some of my thoughts about one major kind of inner reward that often follows living consistent with your governing values: a turning outward to touch and help the lives of others through what I call the Abundance Mentality.

Chapter 11

Organizations Also Need
to Know Who They Are

Like the fundamental ideals of a great nation, church, school, or any other enduring institution, core ideology in a visionary company is a set of basic precepts that plant a fixed stake in the ground: "This is who we are; this is what we stand for; this is what we're all about."
—*James C. Collins and Jerry I. Porras,*
Built to Last: Successful Habits of Visionary Companies

In the sight of the law, almost any formal organization—whether a corporation, partnership, limited liability company, association, union, government entity, or other common forms of organizational structure—is considered a legal "person." As such, an organization has the same legal standing and rights as an individual. But the similarities don't end there. Like humans, an organization is born and grows in its formative years. It may live for a long time, even hundreds of years and in some cases thousands of years. An organization can be healthy or ailing. It may even have to fight for its life, doing economic or political battle with opposing organizations. It can buy and sell things, it can own property, it can be held liable for its acts, and it can be rewarded or punished for those acts. And it will eventually die.

These characteristics are also associated with human beings, and for good reason: Organizations are composed of human beings, and they therefore tend to take on the collective characteristics of those who form them, those who lead and manage them, and those who work for them.

Up to this point, we have focused on ourselves as human beings, each with certain roles we fill in life, each guided and influenced consciously or unconsciously by deeply imbedded governing values. We have seen that the most successful of us generally have at least some degree of understanding of those roles and governing values, most often including a strong sense of personal mission.

Organizations have their counterparts in all this. The roles they fill reflect the functions they play in the economic markets or political structures of human society. Organizations such as a labor union or a farmers' cooperative exist to provide numerical clout for their members and help them achieve the goals of their group. Governmental agencies formulate and administer the laws by which nations, states, and communities regulate the complex interactions of their citizens. Businesses exist to provide income for their employees, owners, or shareholders, generally by exchanging goods and services for money and other forms of value. Religious organizations look after the spiritual welfare of their adherents. Educational institutions educate people, armies and police forces protect the citizenry, and social organizations provide recreation or opportunities for social interaction. Any organization will fill at least one role in the larger scheme of society. Some of the most important organizations fill multiple roles.

Each organization also has values, whether understood or merely implied, that govern to a great extent the decisions made and the actions taken by it. Just as with individuals, these values provide positive or negative influences, both for the group as well as for the larger society. For example, one organization may value tight control of its people or its markets, while another may encourage innovation and risk-taking. Wide variations exist in the personalities and "feel" of organizations depending on the governing values of the group at its core. One government may function within a framework of underlying trust from the people it governs; another may inherently distrust its citizens and keep them under tight control. Some organizations may be altruistic and value contributions to the larger world; others may be self-centered and inwardly focused. The traits that an organization has and the values those traits reveal about the organization are as varied as the vast differences that exist among people.

Almost every organization also has some kind of inner mission or purpose, whether clearly identified and stated, or unperceived. One company's mission may be as simple and direct as "to make a profit," while another organization's mission may be "to save the world."

And, like people, organizations find success or fulfillment in direct proportion to the degree in which they function in harmony with their deeply imbedded framework of roles and governing values, and how well their decisions and actions arise out of their sense of organizational mission. As discussed at the beginning of Part Two of this book, the Constitution of the United States embodies all three of these elements we have been talking about: roles, values, and mission. They are applied to and function in the context of a very large organization called the United States of America.

Coming down to the scale most of us deal with, we find the family, which is defined today as generally consisting of two or more individuals bound together through marriage vows, guardian roles, parental, significant other, and sibling relationships. But like individuals, families don't always recognize that the three elements which lie at the center of individual as well as organizational identity are also at work in their small collective groups. Families could benefit from going through the process outlined in this book and applying the concepts to the family experience. Just as individuals find their lives more focused on what matters most and more fulfilling when that happens, families need to do the same. The members of a family need to identify what their roles are, in both the immediate and the extended family, as well as in the neighborhood and community. A family functions more successfully if its members clarify and put in writing the underlying values that govern or should govern the family, even going so far as to synthesize those roles and values into a simple, memorable, and motivational Family Mission Statement.

This process of discovering and writing down what matters most to a family should not replace what is done at the individual level, and the resulting set of roles, governing values, and Family Mission Statement should not necessarily take precedence over what the individuals in the family have determined is what matters most to them. The family, like any organization, exists to serve the needs of its members and should not override individual values. This generally involves a bit of a balancing act and a lot of give and take, but the rewards in terms of making the family an organization within which all family members can flourish are immeasurable.

A common organization with which most of us have to deal is the company, the generic name for organizations that deal in activities that include the many kinds of transactions of goods, services, and information that make up the economic aspect of life. Here, too, the principles related to the need for roles, governing values, and mission statements are reflected in daily activities. Being an owner and executive in one such organization, I especially appreciate the importance of having what matters most in a corporate sense implemented in the daily life and activities of a company. And I also know the difficulty involved in actually doing that: bridging the gap between what is valued by this collective person called a company and what the company actually achieves in the marketplace or workplace. As an entrepreneur in a small business that has grown to be large and multifaceted, I have been very interested in how some of the companies I admire have been able to accomplish this. In my search for understanding, one of the most impactful books I have read in recent years is *Built to Last: Successful Habits of Visionary Companies* by James C. Collins and Jerry I. Porras. The authors define visionary companies as "premier institutions—the crown jewels—in their industries, widely admired by their peers and having a long track record of making a significant impact on the world around them." The companies they studied were all founded before 1950 and are still in positions of leadership today. The list includes 3M, American Express, General Electric, Hewlett-Packard, Nordstrom, Procter & Gamble, Sony, and Walt Disney. Collins and Porras set out to find what made these companies the way they are and how that helped produce their long-lived leadership positions.

Not surprisingly, the values held by these companies and what the companies have done about them over the years have invariably been major factors in their success and leadership in their industries or markets. The authors note that the visionary companies are "guided by a core ideology—core values and sense of purpose beyond just making money." They also point out that the visionary companies paradoxically make more money than other leading companies in their same field. They go on to say:

> The crucial variable is not the content of a company's ideology, but how deeply it believes its ideology and how consistently it lives, breathes, and expresses it in all that it does. Visionary companies do not ask, "What should we value?" They ask, "What do we *actually* value deep down to our toes."

Then they draw this powerful conclusion:

> A visionary company almost religiously preserves its core ideology—changing it seldom, if ever. Core values in a visionary company form a rock-solid foundation and do not drift with the trends and fashions of the day; in some cases, the core values have remained intact for well over one hundred years. . . . Yet, while keeping their core ideologies tightly fixed, visionary companies display a powerful drive for progress that enables them to change and adapt without compromising their cherished core ideals.

One example in the book had particular meaning for me and, I think, teaches a powerful lesson for all organizations. For more than a century Merck & Company has been a leading pharmaceutical manufacturer. Collins and Porras write that throughout its history Merck and its employees have been guided and inspired by a set of ideals. "In 1935 (decades before 'values statements' became popular) George Merck II articulated those ideals when he said, '[We] are workers in industry who are genuinely inspired by the ideals of advancement of medical science, and of service to humanity.' " More than half a century later, Merck's *Internal Management Guide* restated and reinforced this commitment to the company's core values: "We are in the business of preserving and improving human life.

All of our actions must be measured by our success in achieving this goal."

One particular example of Merck's governing values in action almost moved me to tears. The company had developed a drug called Mectizan that cured "river blindness," a painful disease that infected more than a million people in third world countries. Parasitic worms would get into body tissues, eventually making their way to the eyes, causing great pain and blindness.

There was one problem with the miraculous new drug. The market was there, but the customers could not afford the product. In Collins and Porras's words:

> Knowing that the project would not produce a large return on investment—if it produced one at all—the company nonetheless went forward with the hope that some government agencies or other third parties would purchase and distribute the product once available. No such luck, so Merck elected to give the drug away free to all who needed it. Merck also involved itself directly in distribution efforts—at its own expense—to ensure that the drug did indeed reach the millions of people at risk from the disease.

The remarkable thing in all this is that despite Merck's literally giving away something it had spent millions to develop, the company has nearly always realized unforeseen benefits. After a similar experience giving away streptomycin to halt an increase in tuberculosis in poor, shattered Japan after World War II, Merck went on to become the largest American pharmaceutical company in Japan. Looking back years later, Merck's CEO said, "The long-term consequences of [such actions] are not always clear, but somehow I think they always pay off."

So if an organization, corporation, entity, or whatever it may be is going to be the best in its field, a visionary organization, it must come to grips with what really makes it tick, with what really matters most to everyone involved—employees, owners, executives and managers, and customers. As with individuals, what matters most will vary greatly from company to company, and there are no right or wrong answers as to what that is. But for any organization to be successful and achieve what the people within it want to achieve, it must spin around that organizational nucleus the same three electrons that individuals must spin: roles, values, and mission. Such an organization must seek its own answers to these questions:

- What role (or roles) is this organization going to play in its community, nation, globally, or for its employees, leaders, stockholders, or customers?
- What are the values that will govern the organization's decisions and behavior within each of those roles?
- What is the special mission of this organization? What unique purpose does it have on the planet? Why does it exist, and where is it going?

If an organization is willing to determine the answers to these questions and focus the energy and power of the entire organization on these areas, really see those electrons start to spin, then we can anticipate a similar reaction for the corporation as is possible for the individual.

Understanding the roles, values, and mission of an organization is never more important than when a merger with another organization is being contemplated. Over the past two years I have come to understand that importance in a first-hand way as I have participated in the coming together of the two entities that now make up Franklin Covey Company.

Prior to 1997 Franklin Quest and Covey Leadership Center were two completely separate organizations. Both had developed principle-based productivity, management, and leadership products and had been successfully taking those products to the corporate, professional, and organizational market for many years. Each company served different niches in the market, but many of their clients were the same. As the officers of the two companies began to look at the possible synergy in combining our efforts, it was a natural fit.

In 1997 we embarked on the process of merging the roles, governing values, and missions of these two separate companies into a new entity, Franklin Covey Company. Being a part of that process has been a satisfying and sometimes sobering learning experience for me. It has taught me the importance of clearly identifying the elements that constitute what matters most to a business.

As in a marriage between two individuals, our particular corporate coming together has had its moments both of soaring synergy and frustration and discouragement. From the start, both companies shared many common values and had neatly meshing strengths, capabilities, and markets. But each company originally grew out of strikingly different roots—one from the entrepreneurial world of business, sales, and corporate training, and the other from the more reflective world of academic endeavor. Combining these diverse corporate cultures produced a few bumpy spots along our new corporate highway.

Early in the merger we decided that one of the most important things we could do would be to practice what both companies had been preaching. We set out to identify what mattered most to this new organization, and we took a great deal of time in those early months getting feedback from the entire combined organization as to what the nature of the electrons would be that we would put in orbit around our new company. We spent almost five months working through the process—identifying the roles that we were going to play as a firm, the values that we held, and the mission statement we proposed to live by as an organization. It was not an easy thing to do. The two different corporate cultures had to be modified to mesh with the combined values that emerged.

We first looked at some of the roles the company was filling, including being a contributing member of the community, a competitor in the global marketplace, and an agent for change in the world.

Then we spent considerable time identifying our governing values. After much discussion and debate, we arrived at the following values and their clarifying statements:

- *Character and Competence.* We practice principle-centered living, founding our character on integrity, maturity, and an abundance mentality. We possess technical and conceptual competence; an abundance of either character or competence will not compensate for a shortcoming in the other.

- **Interdependence.** We recognize the value of cooperative effort. Our objective is the success of the organization, best achieved through teaming rather than the building of individual empires.
- **Great Place to Work.** We create an enjoyable, stimulating work environment that attracts and retains top performers. We respect and value diversity.
- **Bias for Action.** We make decisions quickly, not carelessly. We have a higher tolerance for course correction than for inaction.
- **Continuous Improvement.** We recognize that we must continually find better ways to work together. We are willing to let go of what has worked well to find a way that works even better.
- **Customer Focus.** We listen to our customers, seek to understand the needs of the marketplace, and provide legendary customer service. In every effort we undertake, we seek to create greater value for our customer.
- **Extraordinary Financial Results.** We achieve industry-leading financial results, measured by revenue growth, return on sales, and return on equity. Our extraordinary financial results validate that modeling what we teach brings us the effectiveness we promise our customers.

And, finally, we defined and wrote down our mission statement:

> We inspire change by igniting the power of proven principles so that people and organizations achieve what matters most.

These aren't just nice-sounding words. We take these things very seriously. Every associate of the organization has a copy of our governing values and mission statement in his or her planner. We ask our people to look at them often, and we frequently ask ourselves how well we are doing in living up to these values and this mission statement. Are we moving in the direction that we want to go?

This has not been an easy process, but in saying this I do not mean that going through the process has not been worth it. I am confident that we are following correct principles, that the process we are going through is a good process, and that by following the process we have set the stage for ultimate success in making Franklin Covey one of the great and visionary companies.

Interestingly, we have found that, as with individual human beings, there is a gap between our performance and ideals. When there have been difficulties and challenges, in large part it has been due to that gap. But by using the process we have been able to work through the challenges that have come, and it is already beginning to bear good fruit for us. The company is doing well financially and culturally, and the ride has become smoother. I have hopes that in the near future, Franklin Covey will be found on a list of visionary companies similar to the elite group studied by Collins and Porras.

The hows, whys, and wherefores of applying the What Matters Most process to organizations could fill an entire book. For now, just remember that whether your organization has three, three thousand, or three million people in it, the process of identifying what matters most—the roles, governing values, and mission that your organization feels most strongly about—will be one of the most important factors in making it into a great organization, perhaps even a visionary one. When your organization taps into the dynamic energy and power that is released as you do that, you will find you really can work miracles in your organization's particular field of endeavor and influence.

Chapter 12

What Matters Most:
Influence in a Wider Circle

When you have a sense of your own identity and a vision of
where you want to go in your life, then you have the basis for
reaching out to the world and going after your dreams for a
better life.

—Stedman Graham

This is the true joy in life, the being used for a purpose recognized by yourself as a mighty one, the being thoroughly worn
out before you are thrown on the crap heap, the being a force
of nature instead of a feverish clod of ailments and grievances
complaining that the world will not devote itself to making
you happy.

—George Bernard Shaw

In the last several years I have had the privilege of developing a very
close friendship with Gary and Vivienne Player. Gary Player, as you
are probably aware, is one of the best professional golfers ever to play
the game. His golfing record is impressive: He is one of only four
golfers to win all four of the major golf tournaments in the world—
the PGA, the United States Open, the British Open, and the Masters.
Gary has won 163 tournaments in his lifetime career, winning some
of those tournaments in each of five decades. If he wins a tournament
after the turn of the millennium, he will be the only person ever to
win golf tournaments in *six* different decades. But in addition to his
impressive contribution to golf, Gary Player is also a true gentleman.

A few years ago Gail and I had the opportunity of spending a week in South Africa with Gary and Vivienne at their beautiful home at Blair Atholl. While in South Africa we toured a good part of the country and discovered the magnificence and beauty of South Africa.

One man's name kept coming up in our conversations, and Gary Player expressed some powerful feelings about this person whom he counted as a close personal friend—Nelson Mandela. Before our visit to South Africa, I had known of Mandela largely through what had been reported by the news media. I knew that he had been imprisoned for many years because of his opposition to the oppressive apartheid laws that divided his nation's society into two distinct racially based elements for much of the last half-century. I also knew that he had eventually been freed and had gone on to reunite South Africa into a single, multiracial society.

Since our visit I have read more about Mandela and have developed an immense amount of respect for the man, especially for what he became as a result of the adversity he experienced. He was born and spent his childhood in the tribal culture of the Madiba clan in the Transkei province of South Africa's eastern Cape region. He received a good education at local boarding schools, then went on to graduate from college and become a lawyer, working to seek redress from racial wrongs. Mandela became active in the African National Congress, an organization that sought to end white domination and create a multiracial South Africa. As the government grew more repressive, he and the organization became more militant in their views. In the late 1950s and early 1960s Mandela led protests against the apartheid laws, and as the government continued to clamp down, he and the ANC endorsed an "armed struggle" incorporating guerrilla tactics. In August 1962 he was arrested, tried, and sentenced to five years imprisonment on Robben Island, a maximum security prison.

While serving his initial sentence, Mandela was brought to trial along with other ANC leaders and charged with attempting to violently overthrow the government. With the others he was convicted and sentenced to life in prison, and he began serving that sentence in the winter of 1964.

If you found yourself imprisoned for life in what has been described as one of the most dismal prisons anywhere, it would be easy to simply give up or live with feelings of hatred, resentment, and a desire for revenge. Not Nelson Mandela. During these trying years he turned to his innermost values. With time to think and ponder what was really important to him, he was able to resist the temptation to be bitter or vengeful. In his autobiography, written after he had been freed, he wrote:

> It was during those long and lonely years that my hunger for the freedom of my own people became a hunger for the freedom of all people, white and black. I knew as well as I knew anything that the oppressor must be liberated just as surely as the oppressed. A man who takes away another man's freedom is a prisoner of hatred, he is locked behind the bars of prejudice and narrow-mindedness. I am not truly free if I am taking away someone else's freedom, just as surely as I am not free when my freedom is taken from me. The oppressed and the oppressor alike are robbed of their humanity.

He not only identified and clarified his governing values, but he also put into words the sense of mission that was to characterize his endeavors for the remainder of his life: "to liberate the oppressed and the oppressor both." When many people would have slipped into despair and dark thoughts of vengeance and retribution, Mandela retained his faith in himself and in mankind in general. Although it was theoretically possible for him to secure an eventual pardon or release from prison, this was at best a remote possibility. But after his incarceration became a worldwide cause, reform for South Africa and release for Mandela eventually came. On February 2, 1990, President F. W. de Klerk, who had earlier started to dismantle apartheid, announced the lifting of the bans against the ANC and other political organizations. Nine days later Mandela was a free man, and he quickly showed the world what he had learned and what he had become.

With actions clearly in concert with his deeply held governing values, Mandela, as deputy president of the ANC, began negotiations with the government on forming a new multiracial democracy in South Africa. The next year he became president of the ANC, and over the next few years he worked closely with President de Klerk to end interracial violence and establish a new constitution for the country. After being awarded the Nobel Peace Prize jointly with de Klerk in December 1993, Mandela was elected president of South Africa in the first multiracial elections in the nation's history. At the swearing-in ceremony, Mandela arranged to have sitting in the front row the jailers who had kept him captive for twenty-seven years. To me that gesture is the ultimate evidence of a man who knew who he was and knew he was making a powerful difference in his own country and being an example to the world. I get goose bumps every time I think about it.

Even then he did not feel his work was complete. In his autobiography he states:

> When I walked out of prison, that was my mission, to liberate the oppressed and the oppressor both. Some say that has now been achieved. But I know that that is not the case. The truth is that we are not yet free; *we have merely achieved the freedom to be free, the right not to be oppressed.* We have not taken the final step of our journey, but the first step on a longer and even more difficult road. For to be free is not merely to cast off one's chains, but to live in a way that respects and enhances the freedom of others.

I marvel at the wisdom of that statement, especially in light of all the injustice he had endured. He continues:

> The true test of our devotion to freedom is just beginning. I have walked that long road to freedom. I have tried not to falter; I have made missteps along the way. But I have discovered the secret that after climbing a great hill, one only finds that there are many more hills to climb. I have taken a moment here to rest, to steal a view of the glorious vista that surrounds me, to look back on the distance I have come. But I can rest only for a moment, for with freedom comes responsibilities, and I dare not linger, for my long walk is not yet ended.

The world needs more individuals like Nelson Mandela—men and women who can get in touch with the human values that unite everyone on the planet, who can put the power of those values to work in their individual lives to make it possible that, in Winston Churchill's memorable phrase in the dark days of World War II, "the life of the world may move forward into broad, sunlit uplands."

Expanding Our Influence Beyond Our Immediate Circle

For many years Stephen Covey has taught that each of us has a personal circle of influence, a large or small group of people with whom we can make a difference or on whom our words and actions have some effect. Our circle of influence is generally smaller than the sec-

ond circle that encompasses it—our circle of concern. We may be concerned about many things—global warming, wars and famines in the world, the dumbing down of our culture, the increasing lack of civility on a societal scale—but we usually don't have enough personal influence to do a great deal about them. Within our personal circle of influence, however, we can make a difference. Armed with a clearer understanding of who we are, what matters most to us, and what we are about, we can also find our circle of influence greatly expanded and our ability to make a difference vastly increased.

Nelson Mandela provides a powerful example of a person whose circle of influence transcended his immediate family and friends. After he had been sentenced to life imprisonment at Robben Island, those who had helped put him there thought his circle of influence had been effectively reduced to the few prisoners with whom he would associate. Little did they know of the power of the values within this incredible individual. Mandela would be the first to admit that the jury is still out on how well his native country will achieve a just and equitable multiracial society. But his personal influence has at least set his nation on a good road and has brought hope to millions. Without his influence, South Africa could well have found itself in the midst of the kind of interracial warfare that has been tearing apart so many other nations.

Others Who Are Making a Difference in Their Circles of Influence

As inspired as I am by Nelson Mandela's courage, power, and example to us, I realize that he is one of the rare few who has been able to make a large-scale difference in the world. The rest of us may have to be content with lesser degrees of influence. I also believe, though, that our ability to make a difference comes from having clearly identified what matters most to us and, consequently, who and what we are. Armed with a better understanding of our own roles in the communities and societies of which we are a part, with clearly identified governing values, and with our own sense of personal mission, each of us can make a difference in the world. Each of us brings to the world table our own unique perspectives on life, the wisdom gained by our separate life experiences, and our special talents and abilities. Just as a journey of a thousand miles begins with a single step, so the changing of the minds of one family or millions of people begins with the efforts of single individuals—people who, like Nelson Mandela, have gotten in touch with what really matters most and are determined to live in accordance with their governing values in the face of misunderstanding, adversity, or outright evil.

I'd like to help you become better acquainted with three individuals who can show us how to expand our circles of influence beyond our immediate families. I selected these three because they are not Nelson Mandelas or Winston Churchills but ordinary people carrying out their roles in life in harmony with deeply held governing values and a sense of personal mission. In the process they are making a difference within their individual spheres of influence.

Working for Better Schools and Communities

I first heard about Barbara Zelinski of Auburn Hills, Michigan, a couple of years ago when she sent a letter expressing appreciation for having been taught the What Matters Most process and sharing how it was helping her. Like many other young mothers, she had identified her children as some of her most important values. What excited me was that she was really doing something about it in a way that impacted not only her family but the entire community.

Barb (as she calls herself) was professionally certified as a medical assistant but decided to work part-time, first in a dental office and later as a program director with the local council of Camp Fire Boys and Girls. She did this purposely so that she could spend as much time as possible with her children: Sarah, now thirteen; Michelle, nine; and Ben, eight. Not content to be limited to her family circle, in the fall of 1995 Barb decided to volunteer at Auburn Elementary School where her children were students (and the school she had attended as a child).

Armed with a vision that children and teachers would work and learn more effectively in an appealing environment, she founded the school's Beautification Committee. Under leadership described by teachers and others associated with the effort as "quiet" and "behind the scenes," Barb worked with zeal and a penchant for action. Bringing together students, teachers, and volunteer parents, the group planted flowers around the entire school, painted playground equipment, and completely revamped and beautified the school's courtyard. In a newspaper article about her efforts, Barb stated her belief that her involvement "will promote a sense of self-worth and school pride in the children."

In addition to wanting to make a difference in the learning environment of her own children, Barb was motivated by the desire to "give something back" to the community in which she grew up—another governing value. Her efforts have gone beyond the Beautification Committee, and Barb has served as president of the Parent-Teacher Organization at Auburn, and as vice president of the PTO at Meadows Upper-Elementary School, and more recently with the Camp Fire Boys and Girls. She has turned aside suggestions that she become a candidate for the local school board because "it's too political, and I don't see immediate action or results. . . . I'm not saying the board doesn't or can't make a difference, but I want to take an idea and take instant action."

She has found her volunteer activity extremely gratifying, and she says the effort has given her the opportunity to meet many people in the community that she now considers close friends. She also enjoys doing things with her husband, Mike, who works at General Motors, and working with him to "do everything possible to raise happy, well-adjusted children." Amazingly, she still finds time for running, physical fitness, bowling, golf, home gardening, crafts, and reading. And she does all this without the least hint of playing the martyr or appearing to be hassled. In her words, "I enjoy doing what I'm doing."

Her example has inspired others. A kindergarten teacher at Auburn Elementary said, "Her organizational skills are incredible. If you want something done, you ask Barb. She just does everything, and I don't think she ever misses a thing. I wish I could be like her every day; she's my idol."

Barbara Zelinski says her major accomplishment at this particular stage of her life has been "my success in juggling my marriage, my career, my family, and my volunteer work while maintaining my physical fitness"—quite an accomplishment. At the top of her daily task list are those things that matter most in her life, and by so living she has made a lasting difference in Auburn Hills, Michigan.

The Oldest Rookie

Our ability to influence a wider circle of people does not necessarily come from conscious, active effort on our part. Sometimes our influence lies in simply giving inspiration and hope to others. One such example is Jim Morris of Big Lake, Texas. A thirty-five-year-old high school chemistry teacher who also coached the school baseball team, Morris came to national attention in the summer of 1999 when he found himself pitching for a major league baseball team.

Morris had played professional baseball years earlier in the Milwaukee Brewers farm system, but after a couple of mediocre seasons and a few injuries, he went to college and became a schoolteacher. The dream of playing big-league ball never left him, but Morris didn't talk much about it. For many years baseball seemed to be just another part of his past.

But in 1997, after his high school baseball team had suffered through a series of losing seasons, Jim took over as coach. As he worked with the team and tried to inspire them, he talked about his minor league experiences, including the time he struck out a young player named Mark McGwire. He also pitched to the kids during batting practice, throwing fast balls that the players realized were "major league scary." They came in much faster than anything they were seeing from their opponents.

One day after Morris had given the team a pep talk about following their dreams, the kids challenged him to follow his own dreams and try out for a major league club. No way, he said. He was too old. He'd been there, done that. It hadn't worked the first time, so why would it now? The team persisted. In the spring of 1999 they made a deal with Morris that if their team made it to the state tournament, he would go to a major league tryout. As reported in *Time* magazine, Morris agreed, "just to get them to shut up."

His team, the Owls, made it to the second round of the state tournament, so now it was up to Morris to keep his end of the bargain. Hearing about a tryout for the Tampa Bay Devil Rays in a neighboring town, Morris showed up with his mitt. Interestingly, the scout at the tryout had seen Morris in the minors fifteen years earlier. The hour was late, so the scout tried to humor him along. As the scout related later on a radio interview with National Public Radio, "I just told him, 'Don't worry about going to the bullpen and getting loose. Just go out there and get loose on the mound. Let's get this over with so I can get home.' "

So without really warming up, Morris went to the mound and threw his first pitch. The scout clocked it on his radar gun at 94 miles per hour. "I said to the guy next to me—he had a gun—'I think there's something the matter with my gun.' He said, 'No. I got the same thing.' " The scout asked Morris for another pitch. This one came in at 96 miles per hour. Then came another at 95, one at 97, and then twelve straight pitches at 98 miles per hour—a rare speed even for pitchers in the major leagues. In his own earlier minor league stint Morris had never thrown faster than 88 miles per hour.

After spending two and a half months in the Devil Rays' minor league system, Morris was called up to the majors. Going in as a re-lief pitcher, he had three scoreless innings in two games before giving up a three-run homer in his next game. The Devil Rays' coaching staff is upbeat about their graying, near-middle-age rookie and what he'll do for the team in the future. As for himself, he's looking forward to the possibility of being a starting pitcher next season.

The jury is still out as to Jim Morris's ultimate success in the major leagues, but he is already an inspiration to many—to his high school team and to thousands of us who became aware of an individual who followed his dream.

Fulfillment Among the Orangutans

Somewhere between the global impact of a Nelson Mandela and the personal inspiration provided by Jim Morris and his baseball dream is the personal influence of Evelyn Gallardo. A few years ago I received a letter from her. She had attended one of my seminars and had written to report the impact that learning the What Matters Most process had in her life. I didn't know a lot about her at the time, but after learning what she is doing with her life, I have been inspired by her commitment to following what matters most to her.

Evelyn Gallardo, of Mexican-Hopi heritage, grew up in east Los Angeles. Her paternal great-grandfather rode with Pancho Villa during the Mexican Revolution, and when she was very young, he nurtured her love of nature by telling her wonderful stories about plants and animals and the world in which we live. She later loved the Tarzan stories of Edgar Rice Burroughs, and she developed a great love of apes and other primates. "My first crush was King Kong," she says. "As I watched the movie, I wanted to reach into the television and lead this wonderful ape back to Africa. I thought no one understood him the way I did."

Her early interest sent her to the zoo, where she was mesmerized for hours by the primates. What fascinated Evelyn most were the apes' expressive eyes. "I wondered what they thought, how they felt, and how much they missed their home in the forest," she recounts.

For most people such an interest and fascination would be shed by adulthood, when childhood gets pushed into the background and we get on with the more "important" matters of life. Evelyn worked in a variety of what might be called "usual" occupations: file clerk, telephone operator, supervisor at a health club, sales promotion manager for an international firm. Her least favorite job was demonstrating nonstick pots and pans, and a knife that cut through cans.

Through it all, her childhood dreams and fantasies insistently found their way through the bustle of career and family. Finally, at age thirty-seven, Evelyn Gallardo, in her words, "finally decided what I wanted to be when I grew up: a writer and wildlife photographer."

As a child she had dreamed of traveling, so she began traveling— to eastern Africa, most of South America, Southeast Asia, and other places to photograph wildlife. She visited and studied with Dr. Birute Galdikas, learning firsthand about her groundbreaking studies of the endangered orangutans of the Borneo rain forests. From this experience she wrote a book for children, *Among the Orangutans*, about Dr. Galdikas and her work with these endangered primates. The book, illustrated with Evelyn's full-color photographs, became a best-seller, and she has continued her travels and photography and writing. In addition, she has undertaken a large-scale program of working with school groups, teaching them to follow their own dreams just as she has.

Evelyn enjoys her life with her husband and family, as well as her growing activity and reputation as a writer, public speaker, photographer, and conservation volunteer. In her letter she said that her "plate is heaped extra high" and expressed appreciation for the way the What Matters Most process helped her in her focus and efforts to accomplish the things that really matter most to her. She concluded: "My pyramid is developing into a great plan for my future. And guess what? I have inner peace for the first time in my life. Thank you."

How Wide Should Your Circle Be?

As I have said many times in this book, it's not my place to tell you precisely what your roles, governing values, or sense of mission should be. Neither do I presume to tell you what you should be doing about those things, nor will I suggest how wide your circle of influence should be. There are no right and wrong answers to that question. If you do become the Nelson Mandela of your community or country, it will be a reflection of what is uniquely you and the dynamics of personality, aspiration, and achievement that knowledge of inner self produces in you. Likewise, if your internal compass helps you focus on the close association of family and a few friends, that's okay, too. The process will serve you equally well. The important thing is to act on what you now know about yourself and what really matters to you.

Whatever you feel your mission and the extent of your circle of influence to be, you will still find challenges in implementing your plans. In chapter 10 I talked about the Belief Window we each have and how the beliefs we have placed on our windows affect our actions and our effectiveness in life. Keep that in mind as you undertake your own ways of individually and collectively making a difference in the world, and make every effort to "think outside the box." Just because everybody else seems to think a certain way or common wisdom seems to dictate certain attitudes and actions doesn't mean that they are appropriate for you. If everybody acted in the same way, Nelson Mandela would probably have died in prison, Barbara Zelinski would be known only as a great mom, Jim Morris would still be teaching chemistry, and Evelyn Gallardo might still be selling pots and pans. By looking inward we can think anew about our situation and the contributions we can make. As Abraham Lincoln said, "The dogmas of the quiet past are inadequate for the stormy present. The occasion is piled high with difficulty [this was said in the depths of the Civil War], and we must rise with the occasion. As our case is new, so we must think anew and act anew."

It's always exciting for me to hear about people who are following the process outlined in this book—some as a result of having learned the process, others having done it intuitively. These people are making a difference in their families, in the communities in which they live, or on a national or world stage. Some are well known in their fields of endeavor or spheres of influence, but most are ordinary people doing extraordinary things in their daily lives as they apply their governing values and their sense of personal mission to the roles they play. In the process they are experiencing true personal fulfillment and the kind of inner peace we've talked about.

Chapter 13

Life Is Not Set in Concrete

Life, as I see it, is not a location, but a journey. Everything is in flux and is meant to be. Life flows. We may live at the same number of the street, but it is never the same man who lives there.

—*Henry Ford*

Our life's journey is not a straight-line rise from one level of consciousness to another. Instead, it is a series of steep climbs and flat plateaus, then further climbs. Even though we all approach the journey from different directions, certain of the journey's characteristics are common to all of us.

—*Stuart Wilde*

As late as the early 1960s, Great Britain was still dealing with the effects of World War II, which had ended a little more than fifteen years before. Many cities and towns had been bombed heavily during Hitler's aerial blitz. In London, large sections of the industrial East End had been completely leveled by the bombing and were in the process of being rebuilt. Almost every community in southern England still bore the scars of the bombings, including weed-filled vacant lots and shattered walls overgrown with vines. Economically, the country was still struggling, and many working-class families still lived at or below the poverty line.

Starting in 1963 I spent time in England in a service capacity, working often with underprivileged people in the poorer neighborhoods of some of the industrial towns of eastern and southern England. Coming from an America that was enjoying the prosperity of the postwar boom, I experienced culture shock. I found myself working with many families that lived in situations which seemed more like a Dickens novel than the twentieth century. As many as eight to ten people would be crowded into little brick tenement homes that lacked any kind of central heating. Most often the rather rudimentary sanitary facilities were outside in the back alley. In some of these homes the stench of close human habitation was made worse by the presence of the family dog (always a large one). In the dark drizzle of an English winter, with coal smoke pressing down on the streets from the fireplaces of the close-set houses, some of the worst of these poor neighborhoods seemed almost like scenes out of Dante's Inferno.

It was sadder still to see the hopelessness in so many of the faces of the people who lived in these neighborhoods, especially the teenagers. They were old enough to realize that the innocent enjoyment of their childhood was giving way to rather bleak prospects for the future. One of the popular songs in Britain that year was "My Old Man's a Dustman," a rather amusing tune about a father who was what Americans would call a garbage man. A dustman in England at that time was near the bottom of the social scale. In the words of the song, a dustman was a person who "wears a dustman's hat. He wears 'coo-blimey' trousers, and he lives in a council flat." Some of the kids I worked with had fathers who were dustmen, but at least they had jobs. Many other fathers didn't work at all, and in too many homes there were no fathers.

What bothered me most was that all but a handful of these teenagers seemed to feel they could never rise above their surroundings. Few had any hope of being anything more than a dustman themselves. That's what their grandfathers did, that's what their fathers did, and that's what they expected to do. Part of the problem lay in the fact that the class system in England, which was in its waning days, still affected how people thought of themselves. Whatever their social or economic situation, their present status was the way things were, and there wasn't much they could do about it. As far as most were concerned, life was set in concrete.

But England also offered one of the most beautiful and moving examples, albeit a fictional one, of just the opposite happening, at least for some. In London I had the opportunity to see the long-running musical *My Fair Lady*, based on George Bernard Shaw's play *Pygmalion.* In the play and the musical, Eliza Doolittle is a poor Cockney flower girl from east London grubbing a living by selling blossoms to theatergoers outside London's Covent Garden Opera. A professor of speech, Henry Higgins, notices her working-class speech, and as the result of a wager with his companion, the girl ends up being an experiment to see if a lowly flower girl can, with proper training, be made to look and sound like a lady of the upper class.

After much frustration and anguish on both parts, Higgins succeeds in his experiment to turn Eliza into a lady, only to find that he has fallen in love with her. Eliza, in turn, falls in love with Higgins; more important, she has her eyes opened to life and the possibilities beyond the narrowly focused world she had come from but to which she cannot return. Not always sure of just what is happening to her through this whole experience, she still keeps her basic identity and inner strengths, and emerges into a new life that is completely different and undreamed of at the beginning of the story. For Eliza Doolittle, life was definitely *not* set in concrete.

A Journey, Not a Destination

I've always liked the idea that life is a journey, not a destination. It gives a truer perspective. Just as the scene from the window of a moving automobile or train is constantly changing, so are our lives. One of the best ways to see how your life changes is to read a journal entry, a letter, or something else you wrote about your life ten or twenty years ago. Or look at a photo taken of you or your family a decade or two back. Or better yet, listen to a tape recording or watch a home movie or video. If you're like me, you'll find yourself saying things like "Is that me? Did I really look like that? Did I say that?" Because the day-to-day changes in our lives are gradual, it takes comparative views of the same thing, taken years apart, to see and appreciate what has taken place.

It has almost become a cliché to say that the only constant in life is change. Still, it's true; not only does life change and you change over time, but everything we've talked about in this book also changes. This means your roles change, your governing values change, and even your sense of personal mission may change. Depending on your age, you may already have seen how this happens. At age fifty, for example, you may be completely out of the role of being a parent to little children, but you may have a role as a grandparent. If you're in your twenties, your long-standing role as a student may have changed to that of breadwinner. Perhaps you are at the stage in life when some roles are reversed; you may find yourself caring for and meeting the needs of aging parents.

Even among those roles that remain largely the same, their relative priority may have changed. The role of manager, during the years when you are a manager, is probably a pretty high priority. The role of father, while you have young children, would also have a pretty high priority. Though the roles of father and manager may never completely disappear from your life, they'll change in their relative importance to the other roles you play, often depending on your stage in life. My children are all grown, married, and out of our home. It doesn't mean I'm not their father anymore, but I'm not spending anywhere near the time with them that I did when they were growing up. The time I spend with them is wonderful and I take it very seriously, but I also have time to pursue other roles that have value to me now.

Your governing values will also change over time, in part because your roles change and in part because new experiences will bring new insights and new opportunities. Sometimes values change simply because of the stage of life you are in. For example, at age twenty you may greatly value achieving financial independence. Once that is no longer in doubt, what you do with your assets may take precedence. Good health may not be a value fully appreciated when young, but it will become increasingly important as you get older and begin to deal with the fact that your body is starting to wear.

Personal missions are perhaps less likely to change, but time may alter them as well. The more encompassing you have made your mission in life, the more likely it is to remain somewhat constant. My own personal mission to make a difference, for example, has remained constant for most of my adult life, but the kinds of things I try to make a difference about have changed. On the other hand, someone with a personal mission to become president of the United States will need to change his mission to something else once that goal has been accomplished. The important thing to remember is that life changes, and so does what matters most to you. It's also important to plan now to revisit everything we've talked about in the book once each year. You'll be surprised at how much your life can change in that relatively short period of time.

And what if, in one of your future reviews, you find that you still have an important role or governing value that you have not yet made much headway about implementing? Perhaps an experience of my own will help provide some perspective:

As a youth I purchased a bow and arrow, a longbow, much like the one I saw Robin Hood use in the old Errol Flynn movies. After getting the bow and arrow, I got a bale of hay, went to the empty lot next to our home, put a target on the bale, and started shooting arrows at the target. I fancied myself quite an archer, but actually it was some time before I came anywhere near the target rings, let alone the bull's-eye. But what a thrill it was when that first arrow struck the target and stuck in that bale of hay.

A few years later, faced with the perplexities of growing up and coming from a family with a strong religious background, I became very concerned about sin. I worried about how I could overcome sin, real or imagined, and this extended to other kinds of mistakes I seemed capable of making in life. Sometimes I worried that there would be no hope for me. I was therefore delighted when I learned what the word "sin" really meant. I read somewhere (I don't remember the exact source) that the word "sin" comes from a Latin word that means "to miss the mark." Learning that definition changed my entire perspective on my shortcomings. Remembering my experience with the longbow, I realized that when I missed the target, that didn't mean it was all over, that I had lost my chance. I could try again. I could have a second shot.

That bit of youthful wisdom has stayed with me and has great meaning today. Like the archer striving for perfection, we have a second shot when we fall short on the first. We can do it again, we can do it over, and we can try again and again until we finally hit the mark. The important thing is not that we stumble but that we get back up and keep at it.

Life is a process, not an event. We have lots of opportunities to correct the mistakes that we make. That's what progress is all about. That's what growth is all about as an individual or as an organization. If we're willing to take each defeat as a lesson for the next and greater event, we'll be better prepared for that next and greater event.

If we are willing to internalize the fact that this whole experience of being alive is just that—an experience, a process, a trip—then we won't look at the events of our lives as cataclysmic when we fail at something. We can realize that the experience provided important lessons. We'll go on, try not to repeat the same mistakes, and keep working on the process of living. But the process becomes a whole lot easier to manage when we remain consciously aware of those three electrons—our roles, our governing values, and our unique mission or purpose in life—that spin around the nucleus that is us.

The Best-Laid Plans . . .

Several years ago I had the opportunity of getting to know personally the winningest coach in the history of professional football, Don Shula, for so many years with the National Football League's Miami Dolphins. He and another good friend of mine, Ken Blanchard, for whom I have immense respect, got together and collaborated on a book entitled *Everyone's a Coach*. The book deals with the important function of being a coach to people in real life, not just athletics, and is organized around the word "coach," with each letter being the lead-in to a section of the book.

The "a" in the word "coach" stands for the football concept of "audible ready." The high school I attended in Honolulu was too small for a football team, so I never had the opportunity to play the sport, and although I have loved watching football all my life, I have never worn a helmet and pads and experienced what it's really like to be on the line. The audible ready concept is a very interesting one in the game of football and also appears in our personal lives as well as the life of any organization.

In the modern world of professional football, and even in college football to a great degree, the quarterback doesn't call the plays; they are called from the sidelines. The offensive analyst sends recommendations to the sideline coaches as to what the play ought to be. The play is then sent in to the quarterback, and the quarterback executes the play. But what the coaches on the sideline do not know and what the people up in the booth hanging over the stadium do not know is what the quarterback will actually see when he goes up to the line to call for the ball. Only the quarterback will see how the defense is lining up, and his expertise will tell him what the defense plans to do. If the quarterback believes the play he has been instructed to run won't work based on what he sees, he has to have the courage to change the play. This is what is termed the "audible ready call" by the quarterback. When this happens, you will see the quarterback, as he approaches the center to receive the ball, yell out a whole new play based on his assessment of what the team is now facing from the defensive line. Good quarterbacks—the Steve Youngs, Roger Staubachs, and Joe Montanas of the world—have developed an uncanny ability to do that very well.

The same kind of situation happens to us as we face each day. Sometimes the ground shifts under our very feet, and we recognize that our plans need to be reworked, rethought, or redone. If we have that foundation to our pyramid, a solid understanding of what matters most to us, we can better make our own audible ready calls and change our plans accordingly.

The rapid advance of technology during the past few decades has forced many companies to scurry in response to the shifting ground. Some of them didn't make it. Take, for example, the Super 8-millimeter movie camera. At its zenith no one dreamed that the Super 8, with recorded sound and clear motion picture image, would ever go away. But when VHS videotape and videocassette recorders were created, the Super 8 was no longer as desirable or useful. It wasn't as easy to operate; it required powerful lights in order to shoot indoors or after dark; the rolls of film were only a few minutes long; and you couldn't instantly see the film but had to send it out for processing. VHS videotapes, however, contained hours of images, and you could just take the cassette out of the camera, put it in a videocassette player, turn on the television set, and see the pictures. Super 8 movies died quickly, and several long-lived companies died with them.

I was in college when calculators first came out. Before that time the standard calculator was a slide rule. I can remember getting in a line to sign up for the first Wang electronic calculators that were available. How wonderful they seemed. I spent $300 for a Wang personal calculator, and all it could do was add, subtract, multiply, and divide. Today you can buy a calculator for $9.75 that will do ten times what my original $300 beast would do. The corporate graveyards are filled with companies who bet their futures on those kinds of things; they were not willing to keep a close eye on what was happening to the defensive line in front of them and make the audible ready calls that should have been made.

The same is true in our personal lives. When we are willing to acknowledge that changes are taking place and that those changes demand changes in us, then we will realize that we have to make audible ready calls in our personal or professional lives.

The bottom line of all this is that we need to be more open to intuition and to recognize unexpected insights, hazards, and opportunities. There is such a thing as intuition. There is such a thing as listening to your gut. There is such a thing as seeing developments ahead that will have a dramatic impact on your personal and professional future. If you have taken the time to build the base of the pyramid so that you are on a firm foundation of what matters most, you will be able to make those audible ready calls with courage, speed, and effectiveness.

One of my favorite poems is Robert Frost's often-quoted "The Road Not Taken." It sums up beautifully much of what is in this chapter, with the added emphasis on the need to be open to intuition and looking beyond common wisdom or what is popular. In Frost's words:

> Two roads diverged in a yellow wood,
> And sorry I could not travel both

And be one traveler, long I stood
And looked down one as far as I could
To where it bent in the undergrowth;

Then took the other, as just as fair,
And having perhaps the better claim,
Because it was grassy and wanted wear;
Though as for that the passing there
Had worn them really about the same,

And both that morning equally lay
In leaves no step had trodden black.
Oh, I kept the first for another day!
Yet knowing how way leads on to way,
I doubted if I should ever come back.

I shall be telling this with a sigh
Somewhere ages and ages hence:
Two roads diverged in a wood, and I—
I took the one less traveled by,
And that has made all the difference.

Quite often the road less traveled will be the road that you are going to have to take if you are going to succeed. You may have to leave comfort zones. But in doing so, you will feel an exhilaration in the adventure, and you will find that the firm foundation of your own knowledge of who you really are and what matters most to you *will* make all the difference.

Chapter 14

Your Inner Reward:
Living the Abundant Life

Life begets life. Energy creates energy. It is by spending one-self that one becomes rich.

—*Sarah Bernhardt*

How much larger your life would be if your self were smaller in it; if you could really look at other [people] with common curiosity and pleasure. . . . You would begin to be interested in them. . . . You would break out of this tiny and tawdry theater in which your own little plot is always being played, and you would find yourself under a freer sky, and in a street full of splendid strangers.

—*G. K. Chesterton*

We have already talked about some of the inner rewards that come from living your life each day in a way that reflects what matters most to you. There's a marvelous congruency in our lives that is a natural result of having our actions in alignment with our inner values and who we really are. The feelings of inner peace, the outward energy, focus, and personal effectiveness we have at such times combine to create a richness in our lives that almost compels us to share with those around us. This is part of what I like to call "the abundant life."

What does it mean to live an abundant life? It has a lot to do with the seeming paradox expressed in the old saying: "It is only in giving that we truly receive." Living the abundant life means to have everything you need—spiritually, temporally, physically, emotionally, and psychologically—and to help others have the same thing. I'm not talking about abundance just in terms of money, possessions, or "stuff." I mean having everything you could ever want, of the things that matter most.

As previously mentioned, *your* particular mix of roles, governing values, and personal mission will be different from mine or anyone else's. Likewise, my definition of what constitutes the abundant life will be different from yours. I hope you'll take some time to put into words or thoughts your own ideas about what having an abundant life means to you.

In this chapter I would like to share with you some of what the abundant life means to me. Some of the examples are deeply personal, and I share them with some hesitation because I don't want anyone to think I'm tooting my own horn or trying to make people think I'm some great person. A few of the experiences have not been shared widely outside my own family, and sharing them with you now goes against the part of me that feels strongly that gifts—whether of service or of means—should be given in secret. The experiences reflect what I personally feel is an outgrowth of living consistent with what matters most to me, and I realize that what constitutes the abundant life for you is unique as well. I only hope that my sharing will motivate you to find and live your own form of the abundant life.

Giving Away the Apples

I discovered the magic of the abundance approach to life as a young boy growing up with the Polynesian people in Honolulu. One of the wonderful things about the Polynesian people, and particularly the Hawaiian people, is that they will literally give you the shirt off their back if they perceive that you need it. One of the most meaningful definitions of love that I have ever heard is that it is "total acceptance without judging." The Hawaiian people have mastered that in a marvelous way. I grew up watching people share with one another in a way unlike anywhere else in the world.

My favorite fruit has always been the apple. That's unfortunate if you're growing up in Hawaii, because apples don't grow there. An apple in Hawaii (at least when I was a boy) was a rare and wonderful delicacy.

When I was eight or nine, and the Christmas season was not far off, my parents approached me and asked what I wanted for a gift. Both my parents were schoolteachers and not making a great deal of money, so Christmases were generally pretty lean. They gave me several days to think about my answer, and I gave it a great deal of thought. I then went to my parents and said, "I've decided that what I want most for Christmas is a bushel of apples."

They were stunned by the request, probably thinking that I would want some toy or game, or perhaps something to wear. I didn't think my request was that unusual, and I really wanted a bushel of apples. I had no idea that I was asking my parents for a very expensive gift for a family living in Hawaii. When Christmas morning came, it was our family tradition to go to the kitchen. Nobody could go in the living room where the Christmas tree and the gifts were until after we'd had breakfast, made our beds, and cleaned the house. Then we would all march into the living room to see what Santa Claus had left. I remember my anticipation had run pretty high the night before, and I was finding myself getting excited about the possibility of a bushel of apples.

As we all trooped into the living room that morning, I quickly spotted my stash of presents. Sure enough, there under the Christmas tree with the stocking that had my name on it was a bushel box of apples. I lifted off the lid and found that each apple neatly placed in the box was wrapped in beautiful white tissue paper. There was a cardboard barrier between each level of apples in the box, with four or five levels.

I can't remember exactly how many apples there were, but I remember the thrill I felt on seeing them. I immediately consumed one of the apples and offered some to the rest of the family. After all the gifts had been opened and we were free to do our thing, I went out with my bushel of apples and proceeded to give each of my friends one, two, or in some cases three of my precious apples.

A few hours later I returned home, my box empty, the apples gone. Some in my family expressed concern that my long-awaited gift was gone so soon, but I was as happy as could be. Sharing the apples and experiencing the joy of my friends was part of the gift; my enjoyment of the gift was incomplete without the sharing. I've thought about that experience on many occasions. I'm not exactly sure what motivated me that day. I was too young to understand much about things like the abundant life and giving in order to receive, but I can remember how wonderful it felt to share the apples that I valued so highly with my friends and the people I loved and cared for in my neighborhood.

Looking back on it now, I think it was one of my first experiences in discovering the real magic of what I now call the Abundance Mentality: the feeling that comes when you have more than you need and a willingness to share with those who don't have what you have.

One footnote to the apple story: Several years ago I was given an award by the SRI Gallup Company (the Gallup poll people) and was honored by being inducted into their Hall of Fame. My wife and I flew to Lincoln, Nebraska, for the awards dinner. As part of the ceremony I was taken out into the middle of the ballroom, and there on a table in the center was a bushel of apples. They presented the bushel of apples to me, and then the master of ceremonies told my apple story. I had no idea how they knew about this story because I had never shared it with anyone outside the family; I suspect that someone had a conversation with my mother. My emotions were close to the surface that night when I saw a bushel of apples that symbolized how I have tried to live the Abundance Mentality idea ever since my first apple experience as a boy in Hawaii.

Being a Servant Leader

As you know, my own Personal Mission Statement is to make a difference. When my daily actions have been in line with what matters most to me, I have often been able to do that effectively. And in the process I have learned some marvelous lessons about the kinds of actions that can make a difference.

Two stories from my own personal experience will illustrate what I mean. One happened just a few months ago, the other more than thirty years ago, but they will help you understand a simple but powerful concept called *servant leadership*.

In chapter 9 I talked about my own personal bias for action. Whenever I see something that needs to be done, I have this tendency—sometimes annoying to my family—to do it myself or otherwise mobilize those around me to get it done. Earlier this year I had the opportunity to speak in Orlando, Florida, at a national gathering of more than twelve thousand executives and sales representatives of Avon Products, one of America's major suppliers of cosmetics and personal care products. For several months our company had been working with Avon to develop a customized version of the Franklin Planner, and the purpose of my speech was to teach the group about the Belief Window concept to introduce Avon's marketing theme of "Success by Design." I also told them about the new customized Franklin Planner and urged them to pick up a copy at the Franklin Covey booth at the conference's exhibit hall.

At the conclusion of my presentation there was a major break in the proceedings. I decided to check in with the Franklin Covey people who were manning the exhibit. As I approached the booth, I saw a huge crowd assembled around it, picking up their planners. The booth was seriously understaffed to handle this onslaught of people, so I worked my way into the booth area and started opening boxes, stacking planners, and handing them out.

When my Franklin Covey colleagues realized that I was in the midst of the fray and working with them to solve the problem, one of them said to me, "Hyrum, you're not supposed to be doing this. You're the boss." I laughed, took off my jacket, and just kept working. During the next half hour or so I started getting comments from a number of people who had heard my presentation and had come to the booth to pick up their planners. Several seemed genuinely surprised that I would be doing such ordinary work. Others commented that they were impressed one of the founders of Franklin Covey was working on the front line. When the rush was over and things calmed down, some of my colleagues expressed appreciation for my help. It had meant a great deal to them to have me pitch in and work alongside them during that frantic time.

As I walked away from the booth, I thought about what had just happened. Actually, I felt a little embarrassed that people had made a fuss. I had not jumped into the situation trying to impress everyone or call attention to what I was doing. To me, something clearly needed to be done, and I thought I might as well do it.

That experience drove home to me once again the importance of leaders who are not afraid to show the way to those whom they lead, that they should not be too high and mighty to do the same work. Too often the other leadership paradigm is followed—the leader as a monarch reigning over the subjects of his or her kingdom. Such leaders let their positions go to their heads, and some almost become dictators in their companies or organizations.

I much prefer another paradigm—the leader as the servant or teacher of those he or she leads. In this paradigm the leader sees himself or herself not as a superior but as a colleague. In my view that kind of servant leadership tends to inspire and motivate far more than the approach we typically associate with a strong leader.

Previously I related two of the important lessons I learned more than three decades ago while serving in the U.S. Army. I hope you'll forgive me for telling one more "war story," an experience in which I saw the power of servant leadership in a most monarchical and hierarchical institution, the United States military.

On one occasion during my tenure as a young officer commanding a Pershing missile unit in Germany, my firing battery was called to the field for a mock NATO exercise. One hundred and fifty men with equipment, missiles, and all the materials that would accompany a unit of our size went to the preassigned location in the German countryside on very short notice. Winter was setting in, and we established a permanent field site for our troops and missiles.

One wintry night I was walking the perimeter. Because we had nuclear warheads, we had to have guards posted to make sure no one got into the site or was in a position to take pictures of the missiles. As I walked around to these men guarding the perimeter, the temperature was in the twenties, it was snowing pretty hard, and a stiff wind was blowing. Seeing how cold they were, I thought to myself, "There has to be a better way for these men to perform their guard duty and not have to be exposed to this extreme cold." I returned to the warmth of the command shack, got my first sergeant and a couple of other sergeants together, and expressed my concern about the men out in the cold. They concurred that it was numbingly cold and that there ought to be a way to protect the men from the elements.

As we talked about the situation, this group of leaders hatched a plan to build guard shacks at strategic points where the men could warm themselves before making their next turn about the camp. It was about 10 P.M. when we talked about this, and the first sergeant indicated that he would get on it first thing in the morning. But others in the group thought we should do something about it right then. "It's below freezing out there. We have the materials, so why don't we go out together right now and build the first guard shack?"

The group caught the spirit of servant leadership and got excited about doing it right then, in the middle of the night. Keep in mind that in the military the usual pattern is for the officers and other leaders to make the plans and the privates and other enlisted men to do the work. Not so this time. Our little group of leaders went out and got some surplus telephone poles and a bunch of two-by-fours and a whole lot of plywood that was lying about the compound. Then, between 11 P.M. and 3 A.M., we built the most wonderful guard shack you've ever seen.

We sank four telephone poles in the ground for the foundation. We built a platform of plywood with the two-by-fours, standing well off the ground. We built a shed on top of the platform with big windows in which we put some Plexiglas we had found. We put a roof on the shack, strung an electrical cord, and put in a space heater. When we were through, we were quite proud of this Taj Mahal we had built.

The interesting thing was that while we were building it, the guards walking the perimeter on two-hour shifts were watching us: a first lieutenant, first sergeant, and three staff sergeants building the guard shack in the middle of the night. And all so that PFCs could be more comfortable in their guard duties. When the guards found themselves in the guard shack for the first time, being able to get warm, their expressions of appreciation were gratifying to the group of carpenter/leaders.

Word went around the camp the next day: "Our leaders built us a guard shack." Over the next two days we built five more guard shacks, and this time we received all kinds of help from others in the camp. It didn't matter what their rank or position or responsibilities or jobs were, everybody volunteered to build the guard shacks. In our undoubtedly biased opinion, we had the best guard shacks anywhere in the NATO military system.

It was absolutely fascinating to watch the impact these events had on the morale of the entire organization. They engendered a willingness to serve one another. And it once again proved a time-tested principle: "If you serve your fellow beings, things are better, both for you and for them." To me that's part of the abundant life. You already have enough for your own needs; the real satisfaction comes from sharing what you have—time, talent, other resources—with others who have needs you can help meet.

Living with an Abundance Mentality

What we learn from the servant leadership idea is that when we are living our lives in harmony with what matters most, we unleash the power within us. When this happens, a circular atomic-like reaction occurs: We feel inner peace and fulfillment because our own needs are being met. In turn, that fulfillment helps us be more willing to serve others and to help them have a more abundant life. Things then come full circle as we find that with that service our life becomes more abundant still. I'm reminded of the old saying, "Row another's boat across, and you will find that you have also reached the shore." This is part of what I would call living with an Abundance Mentality. Having this mental outlook on life will help you live a more abundant life.

The Abundance Mentality is the antithesis of the other philosophy so common in the world, what we might call the "scarcity mentality." A scarcity mentality suggests that there is not enough on the planet for everyone; therefore, a person feels the need to grab what he can for himself and hold on to it. It seems as though too many people have internalized that mentality. Selfishness and greed are alive and well.

The Abundance Mentality suggests that there is plenty on the planet for everyone. The big problem seems to lie with those who take, acquire, or accumulate far more than they would ever need in order to live abundantly. With the Abundance Mentality I want to share what I have, especially what I have in excess of what I need.

This great principle segues into several important lessons that we need to learn if we are to live life more abundantly. A simple law of the universe says, "The minute we are able to honestly look ourselves in the mirror and say, 'I have sufficient for my needs,' at that point we are wealthy." In my thinking, anything beyond what is sufficient for our needs does not really belong to us. And if I am creative enough to create more than what is sufficient for my needs, the difference is a stewardship that has been entrusted to me. With that stewardship I believe that I am expected to do something that matters, to make a difference.

Let's say I have decided $40,000 per year in income is sufficient for my needs. Through hard work, ingenuity, or good fortune I am suddenly able to create $60,000 per year in income. Theoretically, I have been given a $20,000 stewardship that I could use to help lighten the burden of someone else. You can take this to the extreme. If I have $1 million and $200,000 is sufficient for my needs, then the $800,000 difference given to me is a stewardship to help someone else.

This is not only a monetary concept; it also applies to how we spend our time. If we can manage our time so that we are satisfying the needs of ourselves, our families, our commitments, our career or business, and our churches and civic organizations, and still have some excess time, then maybe we can do something with it to serve others in a meaningful way.

Clearly, I have to take care of myself and my family (including planning and investing wisely for the future); that's part of defining and identifying what is sufficient for my needs. But then everything else goes into making this world a better place.

Some years ago I had the opportunity to speak at a convention in a city in the Midwest. Upon arriving in that city, the person who had invited me took me to his home for dinner. It was located in a very expensive part of the city. We came to a large, electrically controlled iron gate. He pushed a button in his car, the gate slowly opened, we drove through, the gate closed behind us, and we drove a quarter of a mile on a beautifully wooded driveway to the front of one of the biggest, most magnificent homes I have ever seen. He shared with me the fact that the home cost $8 million. We took a tour prior to having dinner. This man had $3.5 million worth of art in the home, another fact he shared with me.

As I flew home after speaking at the convention, I had two very interesting, powerful, and seemingly opposing thoughts. The first was "I wonder if that guy could get by on a $2 million home or a $1.5 million home and do something that mattered with the difference." The second thought came immediately after the first: "But I would defend his right to have that $8 million home; that's what the free enterprise system is all about."

It was on that trip that I started having these serious feelings about the Abundance Mentality. That home may have been what this man decided was sufficient for his needs, and it may have represented only a small fraction of the wealth he had amassed. And he could have been doing—and in fact was, I later learned—some wonderful things with the part of his wealth that was more than sufficient for his needs.

I developed some strong ideas about this, one of which was that you can't legislate the Abundance Mentality. I wouldn't want any person, government, or social entity telling me how to spend my money. That's not right; that's not how it should be in a society where we are free to choose. But at the same time we ought to be doing those kinds of things. I started giving talks about this around the country. I felt very strongly about it and discovered I got quite exercised over it. I also discovered that giving a talk on the Abundance Mentality and sharing what you have was easy when you're broke personally. I can remember times when we weren't sure where the next meal was coming from. But the willingness to share always seems to carry us through those times.

At the other end of the extreme, I have also felt a desire to live the abundant life. In 1992 we took Franklin Quest public. The company had started with a handful of people working out of my basement in 1983, and going public was the culmination of several years of hard work and effort by many. Standing with my family on the floor of the

New York Stock Exchange that morning in June, I looked up at the Big Board and saw our Wall Street symbol, FNQ, come across the board for the first time. Along with the symbol came the opening price: $16.50 per share. I did a quick mental calculation of $16.50 times the number of shares I owned. A chill went through me as I realized that I had considerably more than was sufficient for my needs. At this realization a little voice in my head said, "Well, Hyrum Smith, are you going to put your money where your mouth has been?"

I had a very sobering conversation with my wife and family while standing in the bedlam which is the New York Stock Exchange. We made a commitment to do something with the difference. We didn't need all that we had, and we asked ourselves, "Are we willing to give it away?"

It is probably not appropriate to share here or perhaps anyplace the specifics of what we chose to do, but I will tell you we started in a very specific and planned way to give away the difference. The amazing thing was discovering that the faster we gave it away in trying to help people, institutions, and entities, the faster the wealth grew. The whole idea of casting your bread on the waters and having it come back tenfold is, I discovered, a natural law of the universe.

As I have gone through my life and had opportunities to share what I had, the feeling of personal value and doing something that really matters, especially when nobody else knows, is the most powerful kind of giving. To go into other details about what we did with our abundance over the last several years would violate the basic principle that I chose to adopt, which is to give anonymously, but I would like to offer one example of an event that was a wonderful experience for me.

I was driving home from work late one night in Salt Lake City. It was about an eighteen-minute drive from my office to my home. As I drove along State Street, a major thoroughfare, I found it was relatively deserted, which is unusual for this particular street. I stopped for a traffic signal, and as I was waiting for the light to turn green, I looked over to my left. There in an old, somewhat broken-down automobile was a beautiful family. The father was driving, the mother next to him was holding a baby in her arms, and there were two children in the backseat. It was clear from their attire and the automobile that this family was struggling financially.

For some reason the lights on State Street were not synchronized, and I found myself stopping for a traffic signal almost every block. Each time I stopped, that same car with the family pulled up next to me. As we proceeded, I found myself thinking, "This family needs help. Help them!" Then: "Well, how am I going to help them? They don't know me. I don't know them. I'll embarrass them. How can I possibly help them? I have no idea who they are or where they live. How can I get in touch with them?"

We stopped at the third stop light. The thought came again: "You need to help this family." So I reached in my wallet and found that I had two $100 bills. Knowing I was going to have to stop at the fourth light, I took these two bills and folded them up very tightly. When we got to the next light, I rolled my window down, stuck my hand out, waved at the family, and asked them to roll down their window. The woman carrying the baby rolled the window down, looking at me somewhat concerned, as if I might do some harm to them. I handed the folded bills to the woman and said, "Please, will you use this for your family?"

She took the bills, closed the window, and then I drove away, watching in my rearview mirror the reaction of the couple. I wish I could describe to you the feelings I experienced. Their expressions were heartwarming. I drove home that night and slept as well as I have ever slept before.

You cannot understand the feelings that come from helping someone in need with your abundance until you have done it—and done it in a way that only you and the people you're helping know about it.

Living the abundant life and having an Abundance Mentality is, for me, all about helping people and blessing the lives of others. As I have mentioned, this is a natural outgrowth of my personal mission to try to make a difference. Your own assessment of what matters most to you and your definition of what would constitute the abundant life may be completely different. But I suggest that some of the most fulfilling things you can do are those in which you give of yourself to meet the needs of others. People all over the world are in desperate need, much of it the result of events or circumstances not of their own making. Whatever the source of those needs, people all over the world are praying for various kinds of help. We have the opportunity to provide answers to those prayers. When we feel those promptings to help, let's help and thereby discover the peace, joy, and transformation that can occur on an individual, a community, a national, and even a global level.

Conclusion: You Can Do It!

I know this now. Every man gives his life for what he believes. Every woman gives her life for what she believes. Sometimes people believe in little or nothing, and yet they give their lives to that little or nothing. One life is all we have, and we live it as we believe in living it and then it's gone. But to surrender what you are and to live without belief is more terrible than dying—even more terrible than dying young.

—Joan of Lorraine,
play by Maxwell Anderson

In the opening chapters of this book we talked about heroes and the impact that they have in our lives. I mentioned several who had a profound impact on me. There is one hero I have not yet mentioned but whom I feel very strongly about, and that is my mother. My mother died in 1992 at the age of eighty-four; she was one of the truly great and noble people who ever walked this earth. Looking at the successes I have had, I can attribute many of them to the guidance, direction, and counsel that I received from my mother at a very young age.

She had a unique, simple way of teaching life's greatest lessons. For example, I remember the lesson she taught about natural consequences for our behavior. On one occasion I had done something particularly bad. I don't remember now what it was, but she approached me and indicated that she was aware of what I had done and that there were natural consequences for that kind of behavior. She gave me a very interesting choice: "You can stay home from the overnight scout camp this coming weekend, or you can get a whipping. It's your choice, but there will be a consequence for your behavior." And then she gave me three days to think about it.

That was an excruciating three days for me. It is interesting how I can remember the emotion of those three days. I weighed those two consequences heavily for seventy-two hours. By the time Friday afternoon rolled around, when I should be preparing and leaving for the scout camp, I finally decided that she surely had mellowed by now and would let me go to the scout camp without the licking. So when she summoned me for my answer, I boldly said, "I think I'll take the licking. It's really important that I go on this camping trip." Deep down in my heart I knew her benevolent nature would not allow any sort of licking at that point.

Now this was back in a time when spanking was considered an appropriate disciplinary measure for parents. My mother looked at me with the stern look that only she could muster and said, "That's fine. Then let's go have the licking." She meted out my punishment, and it painfully taught me the great lesson that there are in fact natural consequences for all of our behavior—good and bad.

My mother taught me another lesson that still has impact today. For as long as I can remember she frequently looked me in the eye and said, "Hyrum, you can do anything you want to if you want to do it badly enough." She said it in many different ways: "If you're willing to pay the price, you can do anything you want to do." "Hyrum, there isn't anything you can't do if you want to do it." I heard this so many times and in so many different contexts that I began to internalize and believe it.

Crossing Hanauma Bay

Those who grow up in the Hawaiian Islands learn to swim at a very young age. In fact, the Hawaiian people throw their children in the ocean when they're just starting to walk and let them discover its power. In such circumstances, you learn to swim very quickly out of a sense of self-preservation. When we went to school, we wore our swimming shorts under our school clothes so that immediately following school we would be on our bicycles and into the ocean within minutes of the school bell ringing. That was as normal to us as it was for mainland kids of my generation to head for a sandlot baseball game after school. You grew up in the ocean. I learned to respect the ocean and its power because I was mangled more than once in the gigantic waves at Pounders Beach over on the north shore of Oahu or at Pipeline or any of the great places where you now see surfing movies filmed.

One of our favorite swimming holes was a place called Hanauma Bay. It lies just a few miles past the Hawaii Kai area on the island of Oahu and is a magnificent natural bay. At one point in the evolution of things it was a volcano; then the sea broke through one side and created the bay. As youths we used to go spear fishing there because the fish were so plentiful. So many people fished there that the fish eventually left, and about twenty years ago the bay was closed to fishing. The fish have since come back, and it's a wonderful place to visit today.

The mouth of Hanauma Bay, where it opens into the sea, is approximately three-fourths of a mile wide. Once in the open sea you can fall prey to what is called the Molokai freight train, the powerful current that flows in the channel between Oahu and the island of Molokai. It's a very strong and dangerous current, and I don't think there are many swimmers who can swim against it.

Another subject of our boyhood debates was whether anyone could swim across the mouth of Hanauma Bay, the three-fourths of a mile between two rocky promontories. The water there is probably about 80 to 90 feet deep, and there is no protection from large fish as is usually afforded by coral reefs close to the surface. We would dare one another to swim across the mouth of the bay. When I was eleven or twelve years old I decided to swim it. After all, I had heard all my life, "Hyrum, you can do anything you want to do if you want to do it badly enough." So I went to the left side of the bay, to a place we called the Toilet Bowl, a wonderful natural bowl where the water comes surging up when a wave comes in. I stood on the edge of the bay for a long time, looking across that three-quarters of a mile to the other side and wondering if I could really do it. "Hyrum, you can do anything you want as long as you want to do it badly enough and you're willing to pay the price."

I suddenly found myself diving into the surf, and I began to swim across Hanauma Bay. As I look back on it now, it was probably a very foolish thing to do. There was no one there to help me if I got in any trouble. The swells were quite high that day—probably 2 to 3 feet and sometimes 4 feet. I had no idea how close I was to the Molokai freight train, but I had great determination.

I swam for what seemed a very long time and calculated that I was about halfway across. I was getting tired, fighting the current was becoming more and more difficult, and I was becoming afraid that I could not make it back to where I started, let alone to the other side. At one point, treading water and facing out to sea, I wondered whether I should keep going or go back. I was not sure if I had reached the halfway point and was in a quandary as to what to do. Suddenly I saw a fin gliding through the waves, about 20 yards away and about 8 inches above the water. The experience is as vivid to me now as it was when I was in the water at age twelve. I remember thinking, "you know, it's probably okay to drown, but it's not okay to get eaten." Then I began swimming like never before in my life. I swam in a frenzy, a demon in the water. I swam faster, harder, and stronger than I had ever done before or since.

I got to the other side of the bay a great deal faster than I had gotten to the middle where I had seen the fin. I climbed up the sharp rocks, which was no small feat in itself, but I was determined to get as far above that water as I could. Shaking from the experience, I looked out over the bay. Running through my mind was my own version of my mother's words: "I knew I could do that. After all, I can do anything I want to do if I want to do it badly enough."

Whether or not the fin represented a man-eating shark or a friendly dolphin, or was just a fin of a manta ray gliding by, I will never know. But in my mind I had a great white shark behind me who hadn't eaten for four days and was looking at my white legs in that surf. I sat on the rock for some time waiting for the shaking in my legs to stop and thinking about what had just occurred. I had been foolish to try it. But I also felt a surge of euphoria at the accomplishment: I had actually swum across the mouth of Hanauma Bay.

That was one of the truly great victories of my life. It has been a source of inspiration on many occasions: when I wondered whether I could finish a task that I had started; whether I could get through high school or college; whether I could graduate from

Officers Candidate School; whether I could be a good battery commander of a Pershing missile unit in Germany; whether I would be a good salesperson; whether I could perform well when I became a senior executive; whether I should start what would become Franklin Quest and, later, Franklin Covey; and, once we had started it, whether we should continue, whether we could really make the dream happen. Whenever doubts surge into my brain, I still recall that feeling of euphoria while sitting on those rocks overlooking Hanauma Bay.

Much water has flowed through the entrance to Hanauma Bay in the years since I swam it for the first and only time. That event, clear as it remains in my memory, also seems to be far down on the road I have traveled. While I have not always lived up to the expectations I have set for myself, I feel a degree of inner peace about my ongoing quest to make a difference.

Among the things I most strongly feel have made a difference are the principles I have tried to teach in this book. They will truly help you find out who you really are, what matters most to you, and how to do something about what matters most. I can promise that the rewards that come from following the process—identifying those electrons of roles, governing values, and personal mission, and spinning them around the nucleus that is uniquely you—will make a major difference in your own life. Most important, you will find a greater measure of what we all seek in life: inner peace and a sense of fulfillment.

Of course the desired results don't necessarily happen in a day or even a month or a year. They will come imperceptibly, through little daily victories when what matters most truly becomes a part of your everyday life. When those personal victories come, the increase in self-worth, the sense of well-being, the sense of oneness with oneself are things that no one can take away.

The What Matters Most Process Really Works

If I were speaking only about my own experience in these matters, I would not be so confident in making those promises. I make them in large measure because of what I have seen in the lives of others who have put the principles and the process to the test in their own lives. Let me share with you excerpts from some of the letters that have come across my desk, all from people who have gone through the process and identified and acted on what matters most to them.

Some letters describe how the process has helped them deal with tragedy. One woman's husband died unexpectedly on a vacation trip, leaving her with seven children to raise. In her words, "I never thought I'd feel in control again. Now that I use [the What Matters Most process], I've been able to redefine who I am and where I might like to go. . . . It's given me great peace to set some goals, work on them, and plan a day at a time."

Others have seen long-held dreams accomplished because of the process. Several years after attending one of my seminars, one man wrote and listed some of the goals that the process helped him accomplish.

> Here is a partial list of the things I have accomplished by focusing on my values and setting measurable, achievable goals that are in tune with those values:
> - Met and married the woman of my dreams.
> - Advanced in my career from a computer programming job to a management position [and] responsible for a $20 million budget. More than doubled my salary in the last five years.
> - Completed numerous endurance races including several marathons and triathlons of various distances, including Ironman.
> - Went back to school and got a master's degree. Graduated number one in my class with a 4.0 GPA.
> - Established a savings plan that has increased my savings by ten times in the last five years.
> - Maintained close relationships with family and friends while working hard to accomplish the above list.
>
> Although I have devoted a lot of time and effort to studying philosophies of personal achievement and goal-setting above

and beyond your program, your system was the catalyst that got me moving in this direction.

The letters are not limited to working adults, either. After detailing some of his successes from following the process, a college student wrote: "As you can see, your method is working very well for me now. I feel more in control of my life. My home life is better because my mother isn't always on my case about not getting things done. My social life is better. . . . My drinking has become very moderate and controlled. I've lost 15 pounds already. And I'm headed pretty closely for a 4.0 this next quarter. Thank you so much for your help."

People write to tell how the process helps them make course corrections. One young professional wrote: "When I find my life getting too busy and feel the stress levels rise, I review my values and goals. Often I find that my daily task priorities have subtly gotten out of whack with my underlying beliefs and goals. I respond by making the appropriate adjustments."

Others talk about how the process has given them courage or motivation to do something about long-held dreams. A city attorney wrote: "My courage to take on new goals has been strengthened. I had a vague desire to write a book 'someday,' but felt I really didn't know how to do it, and could always do it later. I have firmly placed this goal in writing, and have been on a new quest to find out all the intermediate steps I need to get there. Your system has given me confidence that by utilizing it I can get that 'lofty goal' down into my daily task list."

The things that matter most to those who write never cease to amaze me. One man wrote about a long-held and particularly "lofty" goal. He "used the [process] for the goal of reaching North America's highest mountain, Mount McKinley in Alaska. Well, [a month ago] I was standing on top of McKinley. The expedition was a complete success! . . . While training for the trip, I used the [process] extensively. . . . The system worked very well at juggling my training schedule with my work and personal schedule."

Still another individual moved halfway around the world as a result of examining what mattered most. Arriving with a foreign postmark, this letter stated:

I am now living in Jerusalem. Yes, that's right, the real one! . . . As a Jew it's difficult to express the incredible bond I feel with this place.

It was during your class . . . that I realized what my values were. I made a decision to move here in 3 years and I began the steps. As fate had it, I was lucky enough to be asked to work on a project here by my company. While I was here, I found a job and took the plunge!

I am out of my comfort zone and it's "uncomfortable" now, but I'm so glad I'm experiencing this process and to have made the choice "to do" rather than regret.

The message I'm trying to convey in sharing these few letters out of thousands received by me and other seminar leaders is that *whatever matters most to you, you can do something about it*. The process works! It unlocks a personal power from deep within that can help propel you toward fulfillment of those goals that have to do with your most deeply held values and dreams.

Now you must ask yourself this question: *Am I going to do anything about what I have read and done as a result of reading this book?* As you consider that question, let me share excerpts from two poems that provide valuable insights. The first is the last verse of "Every Day."

> Oh, one might reach heroic heights
> By one strong burst of power.
> He might endure the whitest lights
> Of Heaven for an hour.
> But harder is the daily drag
> To smile at trials that fret and fag,
> And not to murmur nor to lag.
> The test of greatness is the way
> One meets the eternal every day.

Remember, it's easy to get excited about setting goals and deciding that you're going to do something great with your life. It's motivating to imagine achieving those victories as you "reach heroic heights" and make great strides in living according to what matters most. But the more likely reality is that the sun will still rise and set in the same way every single day, and you must achieve your lofty goals within that ongoing procession of ordinary twenty-four-hour periods. The same mundane things will still need to be dealt with. In large measure, things will not dramatically change in your house, your neighborhood, or in your job. The process will not change any of those realities, but it will change the only thing it can: *you*. It will change what happens in your brain and what happens in your heart. And the decisions your brain and heart will make are what will, in Robert Frost's words, "make all the difference."

The other poem that I will share with you is entitled "The Race," by Dee Groberg. It's a long poem about a young boy who gets involved in a race. He falls three times and ends up coming in last. His father, who had urged him on each time he fell, steps up to the finish line, and the boy looks at him.

> And to his dad he sadly said, "I didn't do so well."
> "To me you won," his father said. "You rose each time you fell."
> And now when things seem dark and hard, and difficult to
>   face,
> the memory of that little boy helps me in my race.
> For all of life is like that race, with ups and downs and all,
> And all you have to do to win is rise each time you fall.
> "Quit, give up, you're beaten," they still shout in my face,
> But another voice within me says, "Get up and win the race."

The big victories don't come to those who are the fastest, the smartest, the brightest, the wealthiest. The victories come to the people who get up every time they fall. My challenge to you is to follow through with the things we've talked about in this book. Discover the uniqueness of yourself. Identify the roles that matter to you. Write your own constitution by identifying and clarifying those governing values. Create a motivating Personal Mission Statement, defining the mission that has always been there but never before put in writing. Spin those electrons around the nucleus that is you and discover the power that comes when real focus and vision come into your life.

I would like to share one last experience with you. It teaches such a powerful example of what we have been talking about and the benefits and blessings that come from actually initiating and going through the processes we have described.

In the early days of our company I found myself teaching seminars almost every week in some part of the world. When a major firm moved their headquarters to Princeton, New Jersey, I was asked to give part of what they called the advanced course. Sales associates at the top of their measuring system at the end of the first year were invited to the corporate training center in Princeton for a week of special training. It was a very exciting thing to be a part of.

On one occasion a gentleman from the Cleveland area attended my seminar. About a year later I received a five-page handwritten letter from him. It had such a profound impact on me that I actually carried it in my planner for over three years.

In the first two pages he related the following story:

> Hyrum, I attended your seminar in Princeton about a year ago. It never occurred to me that what I do each day ought to be based upon what matters most to me. I had in fact been living in the reactive not the proactive mode that you described. When I returned from your seminar, I decided to take seriously what you had encouraged us to do and that was to really identify my governing values—find out what matters most to me. In that process, I discovered that one of my governing values was a good life for my son. When I admitted to myself that that was one of my governing values, I had to come face to face with the fact that I wasn't doing anything for my son. As a result of clearly defining that governing value, I set some pretty significant goals on what I was going to do with my son. In this last year, I have had the most wonderful year I have ever had with my son.

He then described some of the wonderful things he had done with his son—the ball games, playing catch, going to movies, doing things together on a Saturday, things that he had always wanted to do with his son but had never done.

On about the fourth page of this letter, at the top, he wrote,

Last week, my son, 9 years old, was killed in an automobile accident.

His letter continued,

Hyrum, I have experienced some severe pain at the loss of my son, but what I have not had to experience is any guilt.

He closed the letter,

For the first time in my life, Hyrum, I have realized at a very deep level what you were talking about when you talked about the acquisition and maintenance of inner peace.

I still get a lump in my throat when I think about that letter and the life-changing experience that this man had as a result of identifying his governing values and doing something about them—having that wonderful year with his son, having no idea that at the end of that year he would lose his son in a tragic way. Yes, there was pain. There will always be pain after a loss like that—but not having to experience the guilt that so often accompanies such pain, that is a wonderful thing.

I thought about that letter a lot on May 18, 1995, when I received a telephone call telling me that I had lost my own twenty-four-year-old daughter and a two-year-old granddaughter in a tragic automobile accident. It is not even possible to describe the pain of such news here, but I will tell you one of the sweet experiences that came from that tragedy. Several weeks after the funeral, my wife found our daughter's Franklin Planner on the desk in our home, and she thumbed through it trying to deal with her grief. She came across a page on which our daughter had listed her own governing values. She had written her own constitution and had described in detail what mattered most to her. And what she had accomplished in her life by age twenty-four was truly magnificent. She had recently commented in her planner that she was totally congruent with all of her values. What a wonderful way to leave this world and face your Maker. The love and respect I have for that wonderful daughter is immeasurable and a source of comfort and great joy.

As we come to the close of this journey together, I ask you to take a serious look inside yourself. I hope you have gone through the process as I have unfolded it and have begun to feel the peace and fulfillment that comes from living in harmony with what matters most to you. If you have not yet started, I urge you to begin. When you do, events and experiences and understanding will occur in your life that the rest of the world will look at and call miracles. But you'll know what they are: They're what happens when we really decide that we're going to live our lives consistent with what we have decided matters most.

May inner peace be your reward.

Index

About Franklin Covey Co.

Franklin Covey is a leading global provider of learning and performance solutions for individuals and organizations. Their mission is to inspire change by igniting the power of proven principles so people and organizations achieve what matters most.

Franklin Covey distinguishes itself with unique thought-leadership, and a holistic approach that creates breakthrough, measurable results. They create curriculum and thought leadership through the works of Stephen R. Covey, Hyrum W. Smith, and others. Covey is a leadership authority and author of *The 7 Habits of Highly Effective People*. Smith is the developer of the Franklin Planner System and author of *What Matters Most*.

The company provides expertise in: leadership development; productivity, time, and project management; communication and collaboration; sales performance; managing organizational change and employee retention, measuring the return on investment for learning; and creating effective corporate universities.

With 19,000 facilitators worldwide teaching and training 750,000 people annually, their curriculum is carried out through customized consulting services, personal coaching, custom on-site training, client-facilitated training, online training, and open enrollment workshops. Franklin Covey also provides an array of products available in 33 languages to increase personal and organizational effectiveness.

Franklin Covey's proven strengths are:

- **Assessment and Measurement**—Leading the industry in measuring the impact of learning and performance improvement.
- **Consulting**—Bringing the best strategic thinking available and experienced application insight for the toughest and most critical business challenges.
- **Training and Education**—Providing award-winning content and learning experiences in a wide variety of formats including electronic and online.
- **Implementation Processes**—Assisting in the application of new knowledge and skills.
- **Application Tools**—Leveraging leading-edge technologies and tools to achieve desired learning and business results.

Franklin Covey's client portfolio includes 80 percent of the Fortune 100, 75 percent of the Fortune 500, thousands of smaller and mid-sized businesses and government entities. Clients access Franklin Covey's products and services through professional consulting services, licensed client facilitators, public workshops, catalogs, 127 retail stores and the internet (www.franklincovey.com). With 45 offices in 38 countries, Franklin Covey employs over 3,500 associates.

For information on Franklin Covey, please call, write, or visit our website:
Franklin Covey Europe Ltd
Grant Thornton House
46 West Bar Street
Banbury OX16 9RZ
Tel: +44(0) 1295 274139   Fax: +44(0) 1295 264865
email:training@franklincoveyeurope.com

PROGRAMS

Principle-Centered Leadership Week
The 4 Roles of Leadership
The 7 Habits of Highly Effective People
The Power Principle
What Matters Most

What Matters Most for Palm
  Computing Organizers
Presentation Advantage
Writing Advantage
Meeting Advantage
Building Trust

Franklin Covey Project Management

Getting to Synergy

The Power of Understanding

Helping Clients Succeed

Measuring the Impact of Learning on
Key Business Results

Evaluation and the ROI Process

Principle-Centered Community
Projects

Many of the programs listed above are
now available as On-Line Training

PRODUCTS

Collegiate Planner

Premier School Agendas

Franklin Planner

Pocket PCs

Franklin Planner software

Franklin Planner Software for
Microsoft Outlook

Franklin Planner.com

Palm Organizer with Franklin Planner
Software (and for Microsoft Outlook)

Franklin Covey Style Guide

Priorities Magazine

The 7 Habits Coach

On Target Project Management
Software

The 7 Habits audiotapes

Living the 7 Habits audiotapes

Principle-Centered Leadership
audiotapes

First Things First audiotapes

The 7 Habits of Highly Effective
Families audiotapes

How to Write a Family Mission
Statement audiotapes

The Power Principle audiotapes

Helping Clients Succeed audiotapes

The 7 Habits 360° Profile

Leadership Library video workshops

The 7 Habits of Highly Effective Teens
Journal

Managing Personal Change audiotapes

Loving Reminders

Family Workbooks

BOOKS

*The 10 Natural Laws of Successful Time
and Life Management*

The 7 Habits of Highly Effective People

The 7 Habits of Highly Effective Teens

Living the 7 Habits

First Things First

The Nature of Leadership

The Power Principle

The Breakthrough Factor

Let's Get Real

*To Do . . . Doing . . . Done: A Creative
Approach to Managing Projects*

*Daily Reflections for Highly Effective
People*

*Daily Reflections for Highly Effective
Teens*

OTHER FOCUSED SOLUTIONS

Organizational Consulting

Certification with Franklin Covey

Customized Solutions

Electronic Solutions and Online
Learning

International Symposium on
Leadership and Productivity

Organizational Solutions

Personal Coaching

Speaker Services

The above products and programs are the trademarks of Franklin
Covey Co. with the exception of Palm and Microsoft.

About the Author

Hyrum W. Smith is vice chairman of Franklin Covey Co., a leading provider of learning and performance solutions for professionals and organizations. Franklin Covey provides integrated services, products and tools for increasing effective leadership, productivity, time management, communication and sales.

Prior to co-founding the Franklin Institute in 1984, Hyrum served as senior vice president of Marketing and Sales for the Dealer Services Division at ADP (Automatic Data Processing). Since then, Hyrum has inspired individuals to gain better control of their personal and professional lives through values-based time and life management. More than 18 million Franklin Covey planners and electronic solutions are used by individuals. Training products and related materials are printed in 33 languages throughout the world. Franklin Covey is recognized globally for the Franklin Planner System.

Hyrum has received many awards for community service. In 1987, Hyrum received the Public Service Award by the Association of Federal Investigators. He serves on the board of directors and councils of the Tuacahn Center for the Arts near St. George, Utah, and SkyWest Airlines. He is a past member of the Board of Directors for the U.S. Chamber of Commerce in Washington, D.C., and the Children's Miracle Network. In 1992, Hyrum was awarded the S.R.I. Gallup Hall of Fame and Man of the Year Award. He was also honored as the International Entrepreneur of the Year by the Marriott School of Management in 1993. He received the Silver Beaver Award from the Boy Scouts of America. Along with his many community service awards, Hyrum has also been awarded three honorary doctorate degrees.

Hyrum combines his gift for communication with his wit and enthusiasm to bring thousands of individuals face-to-face with what matters most to them. His greatest passion has always been to interact with people, training and inspiring them to become more effective.

Hyrum is the author of *The 10 Natural Laws of Successful Time and Life Management, Where Eagles Rest,* and *Advanced Day Planner User's Guide,* and is coauthor of *Excellence Through Time Management.*

Hyrum's priorities include spending time with his family and horseback riding. He and his wife, Gail, are the parents of six children.

**SIMON &
SCHUSTER**

LIVING THE 7 HABITS
THE COURAGE TO CHANGE
STEPHEN R. COVEY

Living the 7 Habits is a book that could only
be published now – some 20 years after the
publication of *The 7 Habits of Highly Effective
People*, which has now sold over 12 million
copies worldwide. Covey's new book shows
how the 7 habits have touched the lives of
millions. It is rare that any self-help
philosophy has the opportunity to assess
itself, but with the 7 habits, it is hard to avoid
the impact it has had. From running a
corporation to trying to improve the quality
of the individual's life, Covey's new book will
offer vital examples of people whose success
is grounded in the 7 habits.

PRICE £10.99
ISBN 0 7432 0906 0

**S I M O N &
SCHUSTER**

This book and other **Franklin Covey** titles are available from your book shop or can be ordered direct from the publisher.

0 684 85839 8	**7 Habits of Highly Effective People**	£10.99
0 684 85840 1	**First Things First**	£10.99
0 684 85841 X	**Principle Centered Leadership**	£10.99
0 684 86008 2	**7 Habits of Highly Effective Families**	£10.99
0 7432 0906 0	**Living the 7 Habits**	£10.99
0 684 85609 3	**7 Habits of Highly Effective Teams**	£9.99
0 684 87060 0	**Daily Reflections for Highly Effective Teens**	£6.99
0 684 88717 3	**Daily Reflections for Highly Effective People**	£4.99
0 684 84240 8	**First Things First Everyday**	£4.99

Please send cheque or postal order for the value of the book, free postage and packing within the UK; OVERSEAS including Republic of Ireland £1 per book.

OR: Please debit this amount from my

VISA/ACCESS/MASTERCARD ....

CARD NO:...

EXPIRY DATE ....

AMOUNT £...

NAME ....

ADDRESS..

....

....

SIGNATURE..

Send orders to: SIMON & SCHUSTER CASH SALES
PO Box 29, Douglas, Isle of Man, IM99 1BQ
Tel: 01624 675137, Fax 01624 670923
www.bookpost.co.uk
Please allow 28 days for delivery. Prices and availability subject to
change without notice.

About FranklinCovey

In today's competitive environment, the great opportunities go to those companies that can unleash the talents of the most highly skilled people.

Creating a place where they will come, stay and perform is the Great Opportunity of the New Millennium.

Our solutions significantly and measurably improve your effectiveness.

FranklinCovey is a leading provider of learning and performance solutions for professionals and organisations.

We have built an organisation designed to be your 'One Source' for achieving key business results.

for further information contact

email training@franklincoveyeurope.com

telephone +44 (0)1295 274139

fax +44 (0)1295 264865

www.franklincoveyeurope**.com**

FranklinCovey Europe Ltd
Grant Thornton House
46 West Bar Street
Banbury
Oxfordshire OX16 9RZ

Telephone +44 (0)1295 274100
Fax +44 (0)1295 274101

10%off public workshops and application tools with this voucher.

This offer is redeemable in one of two ways:

Ⓐ **against application tools**

call +44 (0)870 600 0226

(mon-fri 9.00am-5pm) or

Ⓑ **against public workshops**

call +44 (0)1295 274139

and, in both cases, quote priority code 777 and our customer services representatives will be pleased to help.

Please send me information about the following (tick where appropriate) and register my option to claim a subsequent 10% discount:

☐ FranklinCovey's **solutions for organisations**

☐ FranklinCovey's **Public Workshop Programme**

☐ FranklinCovey's **Product Catalogue**

Name

Position

Company Name

Nature of business

Address

Phone

Fax

Email

Number of Employees

Insert this voucher into an envelope and send to the following FREEPOST address;

FranklinCovey Europe Ltd
FREEPOST (NH4923) Banbury OX16 9RZ

This voucher is not valid with any other offer, for electronic products, or other non-discountable products.

10%off public workshops & application tools with this voucher.